D0580042

ENVIRONMENTAL DISASTERS

The Kuwaiti Oil Fires

Kristine Hirschmann

☑®
Facts On File, Inc.

The Kuwaiti Oil Fires

Facts On File, Inc.
132 West 31st Street
New York NY 10001

Library of Congress Cataloging-in-Publication Data
Hirschmann, Kris, 1967–
 The Kuwaiti oil fires / Kristine Hirschmann. / Kristine Harper.
  p. cm. — (Environmental disasters)
 Includes bibliographical references and index.
 ISBN 0-8160-5758-3 (hc: acid-free paper)
  1. Oil wells—Fires and fire prevention—Environmental aspects—Persian Gulf Region. 2. Oil wells—Fires and fire prevention—Kuwait. 3. Oil wells—Fires and fire prevention—Economic aspects—Kuwait. 4. Persian Gulf War, 1991—Environmental aspects. I. Title. II. Environmental disasters (Facts On File)
TD195.P4H573 2005
363.738'2'095367—dc22   2004061976

Facts On File books are available at special discounts when purchased in bulk quantities for businesses, associations, institutions, or sales promotions. Please call our Special Sales Department in New York at (212) 967-8800 or (800) 322-8755.

You can find Facts On File on the World Wide Web at
http://www.factsonfile.com

A Creative Media Applications, Inc. Production
Writer: Kristine Hirschmann
Design and Production: Alan Barnett, Inc.
Editor: Matt Levine
Copy Editor: Laurie Lieb
Proofreader: Laurie Lieb and Tania Bissell
Indexer: Nara Wood
Associated Press Photo Researcher: Yvette Reyes
Consultant: Thomas A. Birkland, Nelson A. Rockefeller College of Public Affairs
    and Policy, University at Albany, State University of New York

Printed in the United States of America

VB PKG 10 9 8 7 6 5 4 3 2 1

This book is printed on acid-free paper.

Contents

Preface

This book is about the massive, disastrous, and unprecedented oil fires set in the country of Kuwait during the 1991 Persian Gulf War. In February 1991, invading soldiers from Iraq ignited the fires while being forced to retreat by a coalition of forces sent by the United Nations (UN). The map on the next page shows the areas of Kuwait where the oil fires burned.

Almost everyone is curious about such catastrophic events. An interest in these disasters, as shown by the decision to read this book, is the first step on a fascinating path toward learning how disasters occur, why they are feared, and what can be done to prevent them from hurting people, as well as their homes and businesses.

The word *disaster* comes from the Latin for "bad star." Thousands of years ago, people believed that certain alignments of the stars influenced events on Earth, including natural disasters. Today, natural disasters are sometimes called "acts of God" because no human made them happen. Scientists now know that earthquakes, hurricanes, and volcanic eruptions occur because of natural processes that the scientists can explain much better than they could even a few years ago.

An event is usually called a disaster only if it hurts people. For example, an earthquake occurred along Alaska's Denali fault in 2002. Although this earthquake had a magnitude of 7.9, it killed no one and did little serious damage. But a "smaller" earthquake—with a magnitude below 7.0—in Kobe, Japan, in 1995 did billions of dollars in damage and killed about 5,100 people. This quake was considered a disaster.

A disaster may also damage animals and the environment. The *Exxon Valdez* oil spill in Alaska is considered a disaster because it injured and killed hundreds of birds, otters, deer, and other animals. The spill also killed thousands of fish—which

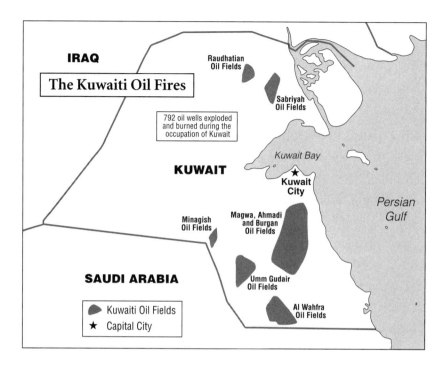

IRAQ

The Kuwaiti Oil Fires

Raudhatian
Oil Fields

Sabriyah
Oil Fields

792 oil wells exploded
and burned during the
occupation of Kuwait

Kuwait Bay

KUWAIT

★
Kuwait
City

Persian
Gulf

Magwa, Ahmadi
and Burgan
Oil Fields

Minagish
Oil Fields

SAUDI ARABIA

Umm Gudair
Oil Fields

Al Wahfra
Oil Fields

⬛ Kuwaiti Oil Fields
★ Capital City

many Alaskan fishers rely on to earn their livelihoods—and polluted the places where the fish spawn.

Disasters are also more likely to happen when people make decisions that leave them *vulnerable* to catastrophe. For example, a beachside community is more vulnerable to a hurricane than a community that is inland from the ocean. When people choose where to live, they are also choosing what sort of natural disasters they may experience in the future; they are choosing the sort of risks they are willing to take. People who live on beaches in Florida know that hurricanes may damage or destroy their houses; people who live in certain areas of California know that earthquakes may strike at any time.

The things that people do to make themselves safer from less dangerous natural events, like heavy rains, sometimes actually make the people more vulnerable to bigger disasters. For example, when a dam is built on a river to protect people downstream from floods, the dam may prevent small floods that would otherwise happen once every 25 years. But when a really big storm occurs—the kind that comes once every 100 years—the dam may not be able to hold back the water. Then a surge of water that is even bigger than it would have been without the dam will come rushing down the river and completely destroy all the buildings in the area.

At first, it may seem easy to blame human disasters, like the *Exxon Valdez* spill, on one or a few people. Some observers blame the spill on the captain, who was responsible for the ship. But perhaps the spill was another crewmember's fault. Maybe the blame should fall on Exxon, because that corporation owned the ship. Or maybe all Americans are to blame, because the United States uses a lot of oil for heating houses and driving cars. Finding the "right people" to blame can be difficult. Is it anyone's fault that people suffer from natural disasters? Natural disasters at first appear to be merely unfortunate "acts of God."

This book and the other books in this series will demonstrate that mistakes people made before a disaster often made the disaster worse than it should have been. But they will also show how many people work to lessen the damage caused by disasters. Firefighters, sailors, and police officers, for example, work very hard right after disasters to rescue people, limit additional damage, and help people get back to their normal lives. Behind the scenes are engineers, architects, legislators, scientists, and other citizens working to design new buildings, make new rules about how and where to build buildings, and enforce those rules so that fewer people will have to risk their lives due to disasters.

The books in this series will show what can be done to reduce the chances that people and communities will suffer from natural and human disasters. Everyone has a role to play in making communities safer. The books in this series can show readers how to become part of a growing movement of citizens and experts that can help everyone make good decisions about disasters.

Please note: All metric conversions in this book are approximate.

Introduction

Environmental disasters are events that cause catastrophic damage to the land, seas, and air. Sometimes, environmental disasters are the result of fundamental forces of nature. An earthquake may trigger the eruption of a volcano that destroys a mountainside or create a giant wave that covers an island with water, sending it back into the sea. Hurricanes and tornadoes may lead to extensive property damage and loss of human life. These natural patterns are beyond the control of human beings. People try to prepare for them, but inevitably are at the mercy of nature.

Humans can cause other environmental disasters. These are usually the result of accidents or ignorance in dealing with materials that humans use in their way of life. Oil spills, for example, are common environmental disasters that occur because of society's need for *fuel*. People study these disasters in order to learn how to avoid similar situations in the future.

In February 1991, the tiny country of Kuwait in the *Middle East* experienced an environmental disaster unlike any the world had ever seen, and it was no accident. In a deliberate act of war, invading soldiers from the country of Iraq damaged, destroyed, and ignited hundreds of oil wells in desert oil fields throughout Kuwait. The Kuwaiti oil fires had a disastrous impact on the people and wildlife of Kuwait, the economy, and the land, sea, and air of the entire region. Almost 15 years later, much of the physical and environmental damage remains, and scientists are still tracking pollution levels and health histories of people in the regions that surrounded the fires.

Oil fires have occurred ever since humans began using oil as fuel. People in the business of retrieving oil from beneath the ground became expert at fighting these fires and bringing them under control quickly, with minimal damage or loss of the

The burning oil fields of Kuwait, shown here in March 1991, spread toxic smoke throughout the Persian Gulf and showered the region with soot and poisonous chemicals. (Photo courtesy of Peter Turnley/CORBIS)

valuable liquid. What distinguished the Kuwaiti oil fires from others was that they were ignited on purpose and that hundreds of wells were burning all at once. In addition, Iraqi forces purposely destroyed many of the mechanisms used to turn off the wells in order to increase the difficulty of repairing the damage. The burning fires raised air temperatures in the desert fields to almost 1,000°F (540°C), shrouding the *Persian Gulf* in a cloud of *toxic* smoke. Earth's oceans and atmosphere were affected by oil pollution, and thousands of birds perished in the disaster. Black rain fell throughout the region, poisoning trees, livestock, and wildlife, and health problems from breathing the fumes affected much of the population.

The Kuwaiti Oil Fires describes how the fires were started, the heroic efforts of the firefighters who brought the burning wells under control, the dire predictions scientists made regarding the results of the fires, and the actual outcome of the aftermath. The book includes information on the long- and short-term health issues facing the people of Kuwait, the resurgence of their economy, and a brief review of the political ramifications of Iraq's actions before, during, and after the war. The book concludes with a time line, a chronology of fuel fires and explosions, a glossary, and a list of sources (books, articles, and web sites) for further information.

Please note: Glossary words are in italics the first time that they appear in the text. Other words defined in the text may also be in italics.

CHAPTER 1

Understanding Oil Fires

In 1991 the Middle East was rocked by an environmental and economic disaster of staggering proportions, covering 400 miles (640 km) of shoreline and affecting the atmosphere more than halfway around the world—the Kuwaiti oil fires incident. Set in motion during the aftermath of the Persian Gulf War, the catastrophe at its worst involved nearly 800 blazing or damaged oil wells. The fires and the *crude oil* released from these wells caused immediate damage in Kuwait and the neighboring countries, as well as long-term harm to the entire region. The lingering effects of the Kuwaiti oil fires are still felt today in some parts of the Middle East.

The burning oil wells of Kuwait raised air temperatures in the desert fields to almost 1,000°F (538°C) and endangered the lives of the workers who fought tirelessly to extinguish the infernos. (Photo courtesy of Peter Turnley/CORBIS)

To understand fully the Kuwaiti oil fires disaster, it is important to understand a few simple things about oil, oil wells, and oil fires in general. Crude oil is a naturally occurring substance that is currently the world's most important source of energy. Crude oil is so valuable that it is sometimes called "black gold." Companies all over the world dedicate themselves to finding, mining, and selling this precious liquid.

Black Gold

Crude oil has its origin in vast numbers of tiny sea creatures that died and sank to the ocean floor. The remains of these creatures were buried in sand and silt. Over millions of years, as the oceans shifted and some disappeared, the sand and silt continued to build up. The buildup created pressure that in turn caused the underground temperature to rise. This combination of heat and pressure slowly changed the buried organic material into crude oil and natural gas.

Oil and gas are lighter than the rock surrounding them, so they begin to move upward through the rock, flowing through any tiny cracks or holes that they reach. At some point, the oil and gas usually bump into a ceiling of especially thick rock through which they cannot pass. They then form an underground *reservoir* that gets larger and larger over time as more material rises from below.

Underground oil reservoirs are the mainstay of the world's petroleum industry. Scientists use a number of methods to find and map these reservoirs. Oil tends to gather and flow through certain kinds of geological formations. Studying rocky outcroppings, soil, and ancient riverbeds, scientists can characterize rock passages that might hold trapped oil. One new method to find oil, called *tomography*, transmits vibrations through the ground that are recorded by a sensor. The data are interpreted and turned into a geological map. Oil companies then sink long *pipelines* into the ground until they reach the valuable liquid. The pipelines are *capped*, or sealed, by control devices known as *oil wells*. The cap covers and seals the pipe so oil cannot leak out where the pipe enters the ground. The world's largest *oil fields* and the estimated sizes of their reservoirs are highlighted in the "World's Largest Oil Fields" sidebar below.

To locate oil buried underneath the ocean floor, special ships use *seismic surveys*. A seismic survey uses sound waves to create a picture of the layers of rock underneath the water. Scientists study the rock formation to determine where they might find oil. If oil is found underneath the water, a large platform is built above the

The World's Largest Oil Fields

Oil field, country	Estimated size
1. Ghawar, Saudi Arabia	75–83 billion barrels
2. Burgan, Kuwait	66–72 billion barrels
3. Bolivar Coastal, Venezuela	30–32 billion barrels
4. Safaniya-Khafji, Saudi Arabia/Neutral Zone	30 billion barrels
5. Rumaila, Iraq	20 billion barrels
6. Tengiz, Kazakhstan	15–26 billion barrels
7. Ahwaz, Iran	17 billion barrels
8. Kirkuk, Iraq	16 billion barrels
9. Marun, Iran	16 billion barrels
10. Gachsaran, Iran	15 billion barrels

reservoir. The platform is like an artificial island in the middle of the ocean. The platform holds the drills and pumps needed to reach the oil below.

Tapping the Flow

An untouched oil reservoir is under a great deal of natural pressure, simply because oil is so much lighter than the surrounding rock. To understand how this pressure works, imagine forcing an inflated pool toy underwater and then releasing it. The toy immediately shoots upward, because the air within it is lighter than the

An oil fire that occurred early in the history of America's budding oil industry is shown in this 1926 photograph of the well at Spindle Top, Texas. The fire raged for 16 hours and cost $100,000 in damages. (Photo courtesy of Bettmann/CORBIS)

water outside. Oil is under the same sort of pressure, but without any escape route, the oil remains trapped underground. The oil will stay there forever unless cracks or holes open in the rock above.

The oil drilling process is designed to create these holes. When a pipeline first links an oil reservoir with the open air above the surface of the ground, the oil naturally begins to flow upward, quickly reaching the well at the top of the pipeline. From there, the crude oil is directed via smaller pipes into holding containers. The oil flow can be slowed or stopped by valves in the oil well. Without these safety devices, the oil would erupt continuously and uncontrollably.

The vigorous oil flow does not last forever. When oil is removed from a reservoir, the pressure on the remaining oil decreases, so the natural flow of oil slows down over time. When this happens, oil wells may be fitted with pumps that pull oil to the surface. The pumping process is expensive and inefficient compared to the natural pressure method so it is not used unless it becomes necessary. In high-production areas such as the Middle East, most oil wells are designed to restrict rather than increase oil flow. If damaged, these wells can no longer do their job, and crude oil is free to blast like a geyser from the ground. This situation is known in the petroleum industry as a *blowout*. A blowout is not only dangerous; it leads to enormous waste of this precious natural resource. When oil shoots up and flows out of a well onto land or into water, it cannot be collected and utilized.

When Fire Breaks Out

Freely flowing oil is not only wasteful, but is also a fire hazard. Crude oil is extremely *flammable*, meaning it is able to catch fire very easily. As one expert explains, "Crude oil is a highly volatile, explosive cocktail which is lighter than water and burns twice as hot as coal."

In an oil fire, it is not the liquid crude oil that ignites, but the oil's vapor—airborne oil molecules in an invisible cloud that hovers over and around the oil source. A dangerous level of vapor builds up in very little time during a blowout. After it does, any ignition source can start a fire. Even the tiniest electrical spark may cause a violent explosion that quickly settles into a steady blaze. This blaze is hard to stop because the damaged oil well cannot be turned off like a water faucet. Gushing oil constantly adds new vapor to the air, further feeding the roaring flames. An oil fire can burn for days or weeks at a time, blanketing the region in smoky darkness.

As blazes go, oil fires are unusually intense. They are extremely hot, sometimes reaching temperatures above 3,000°F (1,650°C). In comparison, a fire in a backyard barbecue reaches a temperature of about 300°F (150°C). Oil fires also belch clouds of smoke, soot, and poisonous gases into the air. Unburned oil droplets rain constantly from the dark billows rising above the flames, coating everything with a sticky film. If conditions are right, much of the oil erupting from the damaged well spreads into black lakes that surround the fire site. These lakes create their own oil vapor that may ignite in an instant, adding to the *inferno* above.

Oil fires, when they occur, almost always break out near oil wells or pipelines. For this reason, they can be considered modern-age disasters caused almost exclusively by human industrial activities. They are typically small in scope, affecting a limited area. Aged, faulty equipment is usually to blame. After 20 years of use, pipes may develop ruptures and begin leaking. Pipes that are poorly maintained can end up leaking oil into lakes, rivers, or forests for months at time. In populated areas, a fire can begin when someone burns garbage, lights a campfire, or throws flammable items into an affected area. Lightning may strike a region that has been damaged by oil leakage, setting off fires that can destroy lives, homes, farmlands, and businesses.

During an oil fire, chemicals that are released into the air can affect people's health. People may experience breathing problems and secondary burns or develop long-term diseases, such as asthma or lung cancer. The environment also suffers from an oil fire. Massive areas of land are burned, destroying the animals that live there. The filthy smoke that fills the sky can sicken birds. Rain mixes with the chemicals in the air and kills plants when it falls. The oil droplets that do not burn up in the atmosphere can travel on the wind and land in the water supply, contaminating it.

Even a small oil fire can carry a heavy cost. Easiest to count is the price in dollars of fighting the blaze. Because an oil fire is too

In Signal Hill, California, in 1955, a 20-year-old oil well burst into flames and threatened to destroy hundreds of nearby wells before firefighters were able to bring it under control. (Photo courtesy of Bettmann/CORBIS)

hot to be put out by regular hoses or fire extinguishers, this price can be significant. Expert firefighting teams, who may have to travel long distances with special equipment, must be hired. These teams can usually extinguish a fire quickly once they arrive, but getting to the fire site is time-consuming and expensive. Also, valuable oil is lost from the moment that the blaze first erupts until the rogue well is capped. The price of this oil must be accounted for. The economic costs of fighting an oil fire and repairing the damage it causes can reach billions of dollars. An area can take years to recover from an accident this catastrophic.

Oil Fires from the Past

Before the Kuwaiti incident, there had been smaller oil fires that caused tragic damage to the areas where they occurred. In 1905, in a region of Russia called Azerbaijan, warring factions started a fire in the town of Baku. At the time, Baku was a hub of oil production. The fire *ignited* the Baku oil fields, plunging the region into a nightmare of heat and darkness that lasted for several weeks.

Oil pipelines crisscross some parts of rural Africa. In Nigeria in 1998, 1,500 people lost their lives when an oil fire broke out in the village of Jesse. A few years later, in July 2000, another oil fire near the village of Egborode devastated the region. More than 3,000 people burned to death in the Egborode incident, and the local economy was ruined. According to a report released in November 2000,

> Months after the fire, the river is still polluted. Many people have fallen ill after consuming contaminated water…. The destruction of farmlands, forest and the loss of fishes, wildlife and…trees have led to loss of income which has made most people desperately poor. Many people cannot even afford to feed themselves.

In September 1997, 100,000 people fled the region surrounding Vishakhapatnam, India, about 800 miles (1,290 km) south of New Delhi, when an oil fire raged for three days before being brought under control. The fire, which started in the storage facility of an *oil refinery,* led to further damage when oil tankers waiting in the port also caught fire.

An earthquake in northern Japan caused a fire at an oil refinery in 2003. The fire took two days to bring under control, and the city of 173,000 people was enveloped in clouds of dark smoke for weeks.

In February 2003 oil refineries in Indiana and New York experienced fires large enough to affect oil supplies throughout the nation. There were no deaths associated with the disasters, but the long-term economic effects of the accidents are still felt.

Spotlight on Kuwait

If one oil fire is so damaging, what might happen if hundreds of these fires burned simultaneously? Before 1991 scientists could only guess at the answer to this question. Such an event had never occurred, and there was no reason to think that it ever would. But during the Persian Gulf War, Iraqi troops began to torch Kuwait's oil wells. In less than a week, soldiers ignited more than 600 fires—about 60 times the number usually seen worldwide in a year.

More than eight months passed before Kuwait's last blaze was finally extinguished. During this time, billions of dollars in crude oil were lost, and other fire damage put a severe strain on the country's economy. Kuwait and the surrounding region also suffered untold damage to the environment and to the health of the residents. Experts are still trying to calculate the final cost of the Kuwaiti oil fires today. This cost is not easy to determine, and indeed, it may never be known. There is no doubt, however, that in both economic and environmental terms, the Kuwaiti disaster was by far the worst oil fire incident in history.

CHAPTER 2

A Nation Ablaze

An American soldier stands on top of a Kuwaiti tank while oil wells burn in the distance in March 1991. (Photo courtesy of Peter Turnley/CORBIS)

In the years leading up to the Persian Gulf War, tension rooted in years of political and economic disagreement grew between the countries of Iraq and Kuwait. Border disputes and lingering issues stemming from Iraq's war with Iran in the early 1980s were just some of the troubles. Many of the most serious problems had to do with oil.

One major issue involved ownership of the Rumaila oil field. An estimated 90 percent of the field lies within Iraq's borders, yet during the 1980s, Kuwait pumped over $10 billion worth of oil from this reservoir. Iraq felt that this profit should have been shared between the two countries because the borders of the field were in dispute. Iraq also objected to the way that Kuwait handled the oil once it was removed from the ground. The Iraqi government claimed that Kuwait purposely sold too much oil at once. This practice reduced oil prices around the world. Lower oil prices, in turn, hurt the economy of Iraq, which was struggling to recover from its costly war with Iran.

By mid-1990, relations between Iraq and Kuwait had reached a low point. Officials of the two countries met to try to work out their problems, but the talks were not successful. On July 23, 1990, Iraqi forces began to mass at the Kuwait border. On August 2, the forces began their invasion of Kuwait.

The international outcry was immediate. Iraq's invasion of Kuwait was a complete violation of the rules that govern the international community. On August 6, the *United Nations* (UN) imposed an economic boycott on Iraq. (The UN is an international organization of independent countries established in 1945 to promote peace, security, and economic development around the world.) Iraq responded to the UN's action by offering to pull out of Kuwait in return for control of the Rumaila oil field, among other things. This offer was rejected. On November 29, the UN passed a *resolution* that authorized the use of military force against Iraq if Kuwait was not released by January 15, 1991. Part of this resolution can be read in the sidebar, "The United Nations Speaks," on the following page. Troops from the United States and other nations, joined together in a UN coalition, began moving into the Middle East in preparation for a battle to force the Iraqis to leave Kuwait.

The UN deadline came and went without any change in the situation. On January 16, the United States and its allied forces

The United Nations Speaks

On August 2, 1990—the day Iraq invaded Kuwait—the UN Security Council addressed Iraq's actions in Resolution 660. The resolution condemned the invasion and demanded an Iraqi withdrawal. When Iraq failed to comply with UN demands, the council passed a further resolution authorizing the use of force against the rogue nation. Resolution 678 of November 29, 1990, read in part,

> The Security Council, noting that…Iraq refuses to comply with its obligation to implement resolution 660…authorizes Member States co-operating with the Government of Kuwait, unless Iraq on or before 15 January 1991 fully implements the foregoing resolutions, to use all necessary means to uphold and implement resolution 660…and to restore international peace and security in the area.

began a massive air attack and within a week had flown nearly 12,000 bombing missions over Iraq and Kuwait.

The Fires Ignite

Iraqi forces in Kuwait were primary targets of the air attacks. Because these forces were scattered throughout Kuwait's oil fields, damage to the country's oil wells was inevitable—and immediate. By February 15, at least 50 oil fires were burning. Although the evidence is not clear, it is likely that many of these fires started after coalition bombs exploded near oil wells.

The worst damage occurred between February 16 and 22, when Iraqi soldiers deliberately destroyed hundreds of oil wells across Kuwait. Iraqi leader Saddam Hussein had threatened this action several weeks earlier in a television interview that aired in the United States and elsewhere. "If the Iraqis were to use oil for self-defense, then the Iraqis shall be justified for taking such an action," he had warned. Troops fulfilled Hussein's promise by using plastic explosives to blow the caps off oil wells. Black fluid began to gush from the damaged structures. In most cases, the streams of oil were purposely lit on fire. Others ignited due to their closeness to nearby fires and explosions. Jets of roaring flame burst into life across the Kuwaiti landscape as the Iraqi soldiers worked to cripple the country's oil industry rather than give it up.

In addition to destroying most of Kuwait's oil wells, Iraqi soldiers released massive amounts of oil into the Persian Gulf. They

In January 1991, hundreds of miles of shoreline in the Persian Gulf were polluted when Iraqi troops dumped thousands of gallons of Kuwaiti oil into the water as an act of war. (Photo courtesy of Durand/CORBIS/ SYGMA)

Oil by the Numbers

There are 42 gallons (160 l) per barrel of crude oil. When refined, this oil yields approximately 21 gallons (80 l) of gasoline, 9 gallons of gas oil (34 l), 4 gallons (15 l) of lubricants, 3 gallons (11 l) of jet fuel, and 3 gallons of residues. The exact chemical makeup of crude oil is different from field to field, so these numbers vary depending on the oil source.

did this by entering control facilities, subduing the staff that worked there, and then opening valves that allowed the oil to flow freely into the sea. Iraqi forces also sank at least five oil tankers that were anchored along the Kuwaiti coast. The liquid cargo carried by these tankers joined the spills in the water from the inland oil reserves to create an ever-increasing blotch on the gulf's surface. Eventually, an estimated 10 million barrels of crude oil found their way into the gulf. This was by far the worst oil spill in recorded history—more than 38 times larger than the *Exxon Valdez* oil spill in Alaska in 1989. (The amount of oil in a barrel is described in the "Oil by the Numbers" sidebar on this page.) Although the spill was bad, it could have been even worse, as told in the "Escaping Greater Trouble" sidebar on the following page.

The Height of Disaster

On February 25, just over a month after the Gulf War broke out, Iraqi radio stations announced Iraq's surrender and ordered Iraqi troops to leave Kuwait. Two days later, U.S. president George H.W. Bush called a cease-fire. The war in Kuwait was over. The environmental disaster, however, was just beginning. Before hostilities had broken out, the Kuwait Oil Company (KOC) had been operating 944 oil wells. In late February 1991, when the Gulf War ended, 788 of the company's wells were damaged. Of these, 613 were ablaze. Many of those that were not burning were gushing rivers of crude oil into the desert.

There was no way to measure the extent of the fires in the days immediately after the war. Experts were not on the scene, and Kuwait was still a war zone—too dangerous to enter. Scientists

Escaping Greater Trouble

The oil spill in the gulf would have been much worse if not for the actions of several quick-thinking Kuwaiti refinery workers. Iraqi soldiers had planned to open the valves to certain storage tanks holding 8.5 million barrels of crude oil, allowing the oil to escape into the gulf. Refinery workers secretly closed the valves in question and then changed the valve indicators to the "open" position. Iraqi soldiers fell for the ruse, and the tanks remained closed.

now believe that at their peak, the Kuwaiti oil fires burned as much as 6 million barrels of oil per day. This figure equaled 10 to 15 percent of the world's daily oil production at that time. The cost of the blazes was astronomical—more than $1,300 per *second*, based on 1991 oil prices of $19 per barrel. This works out to an economic loss of about $115 million per day for Kuwait's oil industry in fire costs alone.

As bad as they were, the fires were not the only problem. Only one-third to one-half of the oil gushing from the Earth actually burned. The rest flowed or rained onto the desert sands, where it formed more than 300 sticky pools. The largest pools were several feet deep and more than 1 mile (1.6 km) across. The total amount of oil in these pools is not known, but scientists estimate that up to 70 million barrels of well oil found their way onto Kuwait's desert sands.

Hell on Earth

Kuwait's oil fires transformed the face of the country. Once a peaceful, sunny desert nation, Kuwait changed overnight into a choking expanse of smoke. Black, gray, and white clouds belched upward from the burning oil fields, creating an enormous *plume* that blocked out the Sun during even the brightest parts of the day. Kuwait became "darker than the inside of a cow," recalled one person who was there at the time. Because sunlight could not break through the smoke, temperatures plummeted. Kuwait City was nearly 20°F (11°C) cooler than normal on the smokiest days.

The scene was particularly grim in Kuwait's oil fields, where thick streams of flaming oil shot hundreds of feet into the air from damaged *wellheads*. The sound of the gushing jets was deafening. "Someone can be screaming in your face, and you can't hear what he's saying," complained one oil worker. Every now and then, fireballs billowed into the air as new puffs of oil vapor ignited. The heat from these fireballs and from the blazing oil wells raised desert temperatures to hellish levels. Measurements showed that the air was a blistering 950°F (510°C) near one big blaze.

Fire also affected the pools of oil now dotting Kuwait's deserts. Evaporation from these pools created invisible clouds of oil vapor that easily ignited when exposed to flames from burning wells. A seemingly quiet stretch of oil could flare up in an instant, adding its own burden of smoke and heat to the environment.

Oily rain added the final touch to the scene. Droplets flung upward by gushing jets traveled on high winds and eventually fell to the ground in a sticky black mist. This mist coated the ground, creating a tarry pavement over the desert surface that covered buildings, people, cars, and animals. The mist also fell into the Persian Gulf, where it added to the *oil slick* already polluting the water.

The Worldwide Response

Responsibility for controlling the oil fires fell to the KOC, which owned the burning wells. The company hired oil fire specialists from Texas and Canada to extinguish the blazes. Progress was slow at first, and experts feared that it might take up to five years

The Kuwait Oil
Company hired experts
trained to fight oil well
fires from around
the world. Before
the flames were extin-
guished, Kuwait would
lose 85 percent of its
oil production capacity.
(Photo courtesy of
Associated Press)

to snuff out all the fires. The work eventually picked up speed as wartime conditions eased and firefighters became more experienced at extinguishing the fires. By November 1991, all the oil fires had been put out and all the gushing wells had been capped. The crisis phase of the Kuwaiti oil fire disaster was over.

While firefighters did their job, other organizations worked to contain the worst effects of the fires and oil spills. Under the guidance of Saudi Arabia's Meteorology and Environmental Protection Administration (MEPA), companies from around the world began the difficult task of cleaning up the oil spill in the Persian Gulf. Early efforts focused on protecting desalination plants (facilities that turn salt water into fresh water) along the Saudi coast so water for public consumption and irrigation would not be contaminated. The next priority was to recover as much oil as possible. Within a few months, international teams had skimmed about 1.5 million barrels of pure oil from the gulf's waters.

Efforts to clean up Kuwait's deserts were more successful. More than 20 million barrels of crude oil were eventually vacuumed from the sand, processed, and sold. Much of the remaining oil evaporated. By 1993, the worst of the oil pools had disappeared from the surface of the land.

CHAPTER 3

Putting Out the Fires

At the end of February 1991, the oil fields of Kuwait were a fiery inferno of oil, flames, and smoke. Putting out the oil fires became the country's top priority. War-torn Kuwait, however, did not have the equipment or the expertise needed to perform this task. Outside help was needed—and fast.

A firefighter with the Red Adair Company gives directions to others working to extinguish a blaze in the Burgan oil fields in Kuwait in this April 1991 photograph. (Photo courtesy of Associated Press)

The Specialists Arrive

The KOC acted quickly. Company officials contacted three Texas-based companies that specialized in controlling oil well blowouts: Red Adair Company, Boots & Coots International Well Control, and Wild Well Control. Specialists from these companies arrived in Kuwait by the middle of March. Additional workers from a fourth company, Safety Boss of Canada, arrived in early April. Teams from other countries, including Russia, France, and China, would eventually show up to help with the effort, but the original four companies did most of the work in Kuwait months before any backup help arrived.

The first oil well workers to arrive discovered a dismal situation. The KOC was supposed to provide everything that the crews needed to fight the oil fires, but nearly all of the company's equipment had been stolen or damaged during the war. Bulldozers, cranes, hoses, pipe cutters, and other well-control necessities were simply not available. Even water was in short supply. Most of the

U.S. firefighters discuss firefighting techniques while one of 700 torched oil wells burns in the distance. The lake of crude oil in the Ahmadi oil field was the result of oil that erupted from damaged wells and, instead of burning, leaked onto the desert floor, forming slicks and pools of oil. (Photo courtesy of Associated Press)

burning oil wells were miles from the nearest convenient water source—the Persian Gulf. Tanker trucks could deliver seawater to the oil fields, but most of these trucks were busy carrying drinking water to people's homes.

Supplies were badly needed, and getting them was not easy. Ships were not allowed near Kuwait until late April, when military officials finally declared the seas to be free of mines, which are explosive devices placed in the water. Cargo trucks could not approach until damaged roads were rebuilt. To make matters worse, customs officials in both Kuwait and Saudi Arabia seemed to be holding up the delivery of supplies. Without the equipment that they needed, well-control teams could do little to fight the fires. By the end of April, however, it became easier to get the necessary supplies and equipment into Kuwait, and work could begin in earnest, at last.

Many Obstacles

Even with the proper equipment available, putting out Kuwait's oil fires was a daunting task. On entering the burning oil fields, crews discovered 613 blazing wells—far more than they had expected. Jets of flame shot hundreds of feet into the air from some of these wells, roaring like approaching airplanes. The air temperature near these blazes was so hot that nearby sand melted into streams of flowing glass. Without special clothing and gear, a person standing near a burning well would cook within minutes. Touching the hot ground for even an instant would raise blistered welts on bare skin.

Gushing oil was another problem. Streams of sticky liquid blasted upward at more than 800 miles (1,290 km) per hour from the highest-pressure wells. At other wells, oil erupted not only upward but also to the sides. Much of the erupting oil did not burn. Instead, it fell to the desert floor, where it formed slicks and pools. These oily expanses flared up, died down, flared up, and died down again. The cycle was unpredictable and potentially deadly. Workers never knew when a seemingly calm oil pool might ignite, instantly killing anyone who was standing too close.

To approach a burning well, teams of well-control personnel had to cross these blazing oil slicks. They did this with the help of bulldozers that pushed piles of desert sand onto the outer edges of a slick. Workers would continue to dump sand into the oil until enough sand accumulated to rise above the slick, creating a surface for men and machines to cross. This process was repeated until the new "road" reached all the way to the damaged well.

Burning oil slicks were not the only obstacle that well-control crews had to overcome. Crews also had to look out for the many land mines and unexploded shells that littered the desert in the days following the war. These objects were usually buried in the sand or coated with oil, making them impossible to see. Workers were uncomfortably aware that one misstep could kill them at any time. As one of them said, "Every day I'm in that field, I find three or four new ways to die."

On the Scene

The blazing heat from the oil fires was the most difficult obstacle facing the well-control teams. Bulldozers, backhoes, and other equipment had to be wrapped in layers of tin to keep their fuel tanks from getting too hot and exploding. People had to wear bulky protective gear, goggles, and tin helmets, and anyone who needed to approach the blazing wells was showered with a constant, cooling stream of water from powerful hoses. These hoses were positioned at least 65 feet (19.8 m) from the fiery wells to escape the worst of the heat, and hose operators worked inside tin sheds. Still, crews regularly experienced air temperatures over 135°F (57°C) for hours on end.

Close to the wells, workers also had to struggle with the crude oil itself. This oozing substance was everywhere—on the ground,

in the air, and, inevitably, in clothing, eyes, and hair. Crews often had to wade through sticky pools 5 feet (1.5 m) deep to reach their work areas. Once there, they were blasted by the crude oil erupting from the damaged wellheads. "It's like a high-pressure hose right in your face," explained one worker. Just minutes after starting their day, well workers were completely coated with a thick layer of black goo.

Above the desert hung a pall of choking black smoke. "Breathing that stuff gives you headaches and messes with your nasal passages. It feels like somebody is standing on your chest all the time," said a Boots & Coots crew chief. The smoke particles entered and settled in workers' lungs. Some members of the cleanup crew were still coughing up black mucus months after the last fire was extinguished.

Firefighters battling the raging infernos found their protective gear barely adequate against the heat and smoke of the burning wells. (Photo courtesy of Robert van der Hilst/CORBIS)

Extinguishing the Flames

The frightening conditions near the oil wells did not discourage crews. They had fires to put out, and they immediately set about doing this difficult work. They used a number of methods to get the results that they wanted.

Water was the most important firefighting tool used in Kuwait. High-powered pumps that could blast 4,000 gallons (15,140 l) of water per minute were attached to hoses that were pointed at the blazing oil wells. This water extinguished a fire by dropping the temperature below the oil's *ignition point*. The sheer force of the water also pushed fuel away from the fire, causing the fire to die out. The amount of water needed to fight the oil fires is described in the "Lakes in the Desert" sidebar on the following page.

In some cases, water was combined with chemicals to put out fires. Liquid nitrogen and dry chemical mixtures cooled and smothered many blazes. Once the flames disappeared, water was sprayed at the still-gushing wells to cool them further and ensure that the oil would not reignite.

Explosives were another important firefighting tool used when water was not effective. After evaluating the sizes of individual oil fires, workers built custom charges weighing up to 300 pounds (136 kg). Cranes were used to dangle these charges near the mouths of burning oil wells. The charges were then set off, causing powerful explosions. These explosions killed fires in two ways. First, they blasted oil and vapor away from the wells, thus removing the flames' fuel source. Second, they ate up all the oxygen in the air near the wells. Fire cannot burn without oxygen, so even large blazes blinked out quickly in the aftermath of an explosion.

A final method used by the firefighters was called "stinging in." In this method, mud was injected into a gushing well. Over time, enough mud built up to block the erupting oil. Stopping the oil from flowing also stopped the fire above.

Lakes in the Desert

Enormous amounts of water were needed to fight Kuwait's oil fires. To get the needed supplies, vast pits were dug in the desert and then filled with seawater. Bechtel Corporation, the company in charge of this operation, dug more than 300 lagoons in the Kuwaiti desert. Each lagoon could hold between 500,000 and 1 million gallons (1.9 million and 3.8 million l) of water. About 250 miles (400 km) of pipeline were needed to bring this water from the gulf to the fire sites. Together, the various lines sucked water from the gulf at a rate of about 25 million gallons (94.6 million l) per day.

Extinguishing oil well fires was only part of the job. After a fire was put out, crews had to cap the damaged well to stop oil from escaping. This work was difficult because fresh caps are designed to fit over cleanly cut pipes; most of the Kuwaiti well pipes were twisted and broken. This problem had to be solved before a well could be sealed. To cleanly cut a broken pipe, well-control workers used tools called *jet cutters* that blasted out a high-pressure stream of water and sand. This abrasive stream easily sawed through bolts and pipes. Once the damaged parts were gone, workers could clamp new caps onto the pipe heads.

Success at Last

The time needed to extinguish and cap a well could vary. Some small wells were not badly damaged and could be shut off in a few minutes with a simple wrench. Other wells spewed so much oil and flame that they were nearly impossible to fix. For example, it took several weeks and a great deal of trial and error to put out a fire at a pump called Ahmadi 120. This gusher was losing 1,000 gallons (3,780 l) a minute and fueled one of the worst blazes to rage in the aftermath of the Gulf War.

Success came slowly at first. Lacking both experience and supplies, crews from all companies struggled to make progress, but the well-control specialists got better at their work as time passed. By early September, five months after the firefighting effort began, crews had capped half of Kuwait's damaged oil wells. Just two months after that, the job was completed. On November 7,

By August 1991, oil field workers were laying pipe in the Ahmadi oil field to carry crude oil from the well after the fires were extinguished. Firefighters were able to bring the fires under control months earlier than expected, enabling the Kuwaiti oil industry and the country's economy to reestablish themselves. (Photo courtesy of Associated Press)

1991, the *emir* (leader) of Kuwait flipped a ceremonial switch that extinguished the country's last oil well blaze. Nine months of hell were finally over.

In the final accounting, putting out Kuwait's fires was an expensive enterprise. The KOC spent an estimated $2 billion to hire the well-control crews that put out the fires, and another $12 billion worth of crude oil spilled onto the desert sands. There were also human costs: Five workers lost their lives in oil-slick fires, one worker died after stepping on a land mine, and another was run over by a bulldozer. In addition, several workers were severely burned.

These expenses were just the beginning. The cleanup of Kuwait's landscape loomed, and it promised to be costly. Well fires had left the country's deserts soaked in oil and soot and had dumped untold gallons of poison into the Persian Gulf. The fires had killed thousands of animals and torched acres of plants. The nation's petroleum industry was in shambles. Also, residents of Kuwait and the surrounding countries were worried about the long-term health effects of the smoke and oil that they had breathed and touched. What terrors might lurk in Kuwait's future? Because the world had never experienced an oil fire disaster on the scale of the Kuwaiti disaster, no one was able to answer this question. The only solution was to wait, work, and hope for the best.

CHAPTER 4

Immediate Effects and Cleanup

An Iraqi tank stands destroyed and abandoned after coalition forces drove the Iraqi army from Kuwait. An oil well burns in the background, evidence of the heinous act of war ordered by former Iraqi president Saddam Hussein. (Photo courtesy of Associated Press)

In mid-February 1991, smoke began billowing from Kuwait's torched oil wells. The smoke from individual wells rose into the atmosphere, where it merged into one thick plume. "Seen from above, [the plume] assumed every conceivable shape, sometimes smooth, sometimes wavy or puffy; seen from below...it was usually flat, like a ceiling, and black," explained writer T.M. Hawley.

Within days, the plume had spread and thickened enough to plunge parts of Kuwait into perpetual night. Lights had to be turned on at noon, and daytime temperatures plunged as the smoky skies blocked the Sun's rays.

The situation looked bad enough from the ground. Only by rising above the plume, however, was it possible to understand the full impact of the oil fires. Badria al-Awadi, Kuwait's representative to the International Union for the Conservation of Nature, was visibly shaken after her first helicopter ride over the blazes. "You cannot imagine it is like that," she said. "They show only a little burning oil on TV. The international community should see this as something very, very disastrous."

Satellite images gave the world a better picture of the damage. Clearly visible from space, the black pall rising from Kuwait's oil fields spread hundreds of miles to the south and southeast. The smoke drifted over parts of Iran, Iraq, Saudi Arabia, and even distant Yemen. Set atop the United States, the plume would have stretched from New England to Florida.

Air Pollution

Air quality was the biggest concern in the days after the oil fires ignited. In some places, people could see soot swirling in the air at ground level. With every breath, they inhaled this smoky mixture of air and *pollutants* into their lungs. In the words of Brent Blackwelder, vice president for policy of the U.S. environmental organization Friends of the Earth, "With unfavorable wind conditions, the smoke people are breathing is not unlike putting your head over a barbecue pit or like standing behind the exhaust pipes of hundreds of malfunctioning diesel trucks." Some doctors reported that asthma attacks and other respiratory problems skyrocketed when the plume hovered near ground level.

Luckily for Kuwait's residents, this did not occur too often. On most days, the smoke rose several hundred feet before leveling off and drifting downwind. As the plume passed over heavily populated Kuwait City, a combination of weather conditions kept it high in the air rather than pushing it toward the ground, where it could do maximum harm. The days may have been dark and dreary, but at least the air was breathable—most of the time. If the air got too smoky, residents simply shut themselves inside their homes and waited for it to clear up, which it always did before long.

Visible smoke was not the only issue. Scientists believed that dangerous but invisible gases such as hydrogen sulfide, sulfur dioxide, nitrogen oxide, carbon monoxide, and ozone were forming as Kuwait's fires burned. The scientists were afraid that these gases might be floating near ground level, where they could make people very sick. In the days immediately after the war, monitors that could measure these and other pollutants were not available. No one knew how bad the pollution really was or what long-term effects it might have on the people of Kuwait.

Yet another concern was worldwide pollution. At the height of the oil fires, black rain fell hundreds of miles away in Saudi Arabia and Iran. Oil-streaked snow fell in Turkey, hundreds of miles to the northwest of Kuwait. Researchers at Hawaii's Mauna Loa Observatory, about 8,500 miles (13,680 km) from Kuwait's blazing deserts, found traces of oily smoke in the lush tropical skies. This discovery proved that at least some of the air pollution created in Kuwait was finding its way around the world. Scientists worried that Earth's climate might be affected if the oil fires spewed enough smoke into the atmosphere.

Acid rain was a greater issue locally. Acid rain is created after sulfur dioxide and nitrogen oxides are released into the air. These gases react with sunlight, water vapor, wind, and oxygen to create airborne acid droplets. The liquid acid may drift hundreds of miles before washing out of the air and falling to Earth as acid rain. On the ground, it damages plants and changes the chemical makeup of soil. In Iran, Pakistan, Afghanistan, and the southern Soviet Union, acid rain in the wake of the Kuwaiti oil fires was "very severe," said Ruman Bojkov of the World Meteorological Organization (WMO). "The people…don't see anything, they don't feel anything. But when the rain is falling, their crop is damaged."

Oil Everywhere

Wherever the smoke plume drifted, oil was sure to follow. All through the spring and early summer of 1991, a sticky mixture of oil and soot drizzled constantly from Kuwait's black skies. Anyone who ventured outside was soon speckled with tiny black dots, and people who had to spend a lot of time outdoors were coated with the falling oil. The fur and feathers of livestock and wild animals were matted with filth; plants were coated with grime. Unable to take in the air that they needed to survive, many of these plants

Soot (the black and gray shadow in the center of this image) from the oil fires in the Al Buroan and Umm Gudair oil fields settled over the desert, but prevailing winds spared the city of Kuwait to the north. (Photo courtesy of CORBIS)

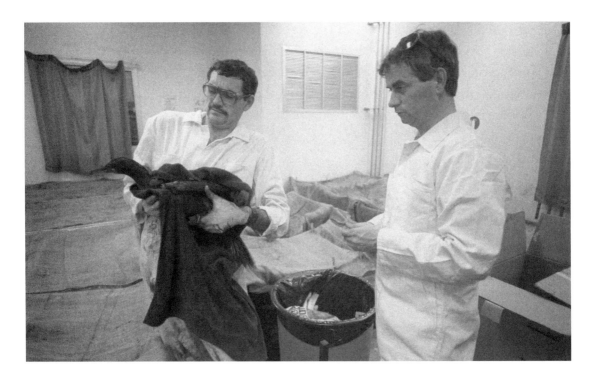

Thousands of shorebirds were poisoned by the oil dumped into the Persian Gulf by Iraqi troops. Volunteers from the National Commission for Wildlife Conservation and Development aided in rescue efforts to save any birds found still alive along the shoreline. (Photo courtesy of Greg E. Mathieson/MAI/Landov)

died. Desperately hungry animals ate other plants and quickly became sick from the oil in their systems. Camels, chickens, desert rodents, lizards, insects, and many other creatures died in droves from starvation, oil poisoning, or a combination of the two.

Oil and soot also affected the land. In some areas, oily rain from the plume left a thin coating that hardened into a dark *tar mat*. In other areas, freely flowing oil created shiny black lakes. Together, the lakes and the tar mats blanketed nearly 700 square miles (1,810 km^2) of land.

Both the tar mats and the oil lakes harmed Kuwait's ecosystem. The tar mats killed plants and ruined the homes of ground-dwelling animals and insects. The lakes poisoned the desert sand and drowned birds, insects, and wild and domestic animals. The lakes and tar mats also added to Kuwait's air pollution burden through evaporation. Crude oil evaporates quickly when exposed to air. Fumes and dangerous chemicals escaped constantly from the oil lakes, tainting the air for miles around.

Drizzling oil also created problems in the Persian Gulf, where fallout from the fires left a colorful sheen on the water's surface. This sheen soon sank into the depths, where it coated sand, coral, plants, and animals. Although not as damaging as the massive slick already poisoning the Gulf, this new oil did add to the sea's pollution burden. Turtles, shrimp, and some fish species were just a few of the creatures affected by the greasy shower. Seashore animals such as crabs and birds also died as oil-soaked waves coated Kuwait and Saudi beaches with tar. By the time the crisis ended, more than 400 miles (640 km) of shoreline had been blackened by oil.

Cleaning it Up

Short of putting out the fires, little could be done about Kuwait's air pollution problem. Cleanup crews could, however, do something about the crude oil that was spilling across the region's seas and land. Early efforts therefore focused on this aspect of the disaster.

The first task was to protect desalination plants along the Saudi coast. These plants took seawater and turned it into fresh water for drinking, bathing, and irrigation. Because they were considered essential to public health, the desalination plants took priority over the environment. MEPA of Saudi Arabia, the organization in charge of cleaning up the spill in the gulf, dropped miles of *booms* (long, flexible, floating plastic tubes used to contain floating oil) into the sea around these facilities. Meanwhile, beaches were closed to the public, but they were not cleaned of oil. Unpopulated areas of the region were also left untreated. MEPA simply did not have enough resources or time to protect these areas.

The next item on the cleanup agenda was recovery of the spilled oil. This was done in several ways. Boats called *skimmers* slurped oil up at sea. Oil floating near land was collected with

Unfortunately, the environment was last on Kuwait's list of priorities in cleaning up the oil spilled by Iraqi troops. This 1991 photograph shows part of a beach covered in oil. Today, much of that oil remains, although some has dispersed through natural processes. (Photo courtesy of Durand/CORBIS/ SYGMA)

gigantic vacuums set along the shoreline. Kuwait's oil pools were sucked into specially equipped vacuum trucks. The recovered oil was stored in enormous holding tanks. Then the tanks were moved in trucks to refineries, where the oil was treated to remove salt water, sand, and other impurities. In the end, an estimated 18 to 24 percent of the oil in the gulf and up to 95 percent of the oil in Kuwait's deserts was recovered and refined.

As the oil fires were brought under control and the recovery of spilled oil proceeded, people finally started turning their attention to the environment. The International Maritime Organization (IMO) spearheaded efforts to clean up sea turtle nesting islands and protect salt marshes. Other organizations worked to remove oil from the beaches of Kuwait and Saudi Arabia, but these efforts were small in scale and tended to move slowly. Money was scarce, and the cleanup methods themselves were controversial. Many scientists believe that cleanup techniques for oil spills do more damage to the environment than the oil itself. Chemicals called *dispersants* are sometimes used to dissolve oil floating in the sea, but the long-term effects of dispersants on marine life and the water are not known. Another cleanup method is using high-powered hoses to shoot hot water over oil accumulated on rocks and sand along the coastline. Water temperatures can increase as a result, damaging fragile plant life and the animals that feed off the plants. Perhaps because of controversy over these methods, the worldwide response to environmentalists' pleas for help was lukewarm at best.

The volunteer-based Jubayl Wildlife Rescue Project in Saudi Arabia made a significant effort to help. Soldiers, doctors, and concerned citizens pitched in to bathe and nurse oil-soaked birds. The volunteers attracted a lot of publicity, and they did good work. More than 1,000 birds were eventually cleaned and released. But this was a tiny number compared to the estimated 40,000 birds that died as a result of Kuwait's oil fires. Scientists do not know how many of the released birds died from internal oil poisoning or stress in the months after their release. Additionally, cleaning birds and other animals was enormously expensive, as related in the "Worth the Cost?" sidebar below.

Worth the Cost?

In the wake of the 1989 *Exxon Valdez* oil spill, workers pioneered techniques for cleaning oil-soaked birds and other animals. These techniques, including gentle scrubbing with detergents, administration of special hydrating drinks, and weeks of rehabilitation, do work. They offer seemingly doomed animals a chance at survival—but at what cost? Experts estimate that the labor, facilities, and medical supplies needed to mount a wildlife rescue operation for otters after the *Exxon Valdez* oil spill carried a price tag of more than $80,000 for each animal saved. The cost of saving the birds at the Jubayl Wildlife Rescue Project was similarly high. Saving oiled animals is undoubtedly good public relations, but many people question whether the results justify the enormous price.

Efforts End but Damage Remains

The efforts at Jubayl were not typical. Most other well-meaning people and organizations could not raise enough money to pay for the work. Without funds, even the most concerned environmentalists could not carry out their cleanup plans. One by one, companies began to give up and trickle out of the Middle East. By the time that the last oil fire was extinguished in November 1991, only $150 million had been contributed to environmental causes, and most cleanup workers were gone. The immediate efforts to salvage the area's environment were basically over.

The impact of the Kuwaiti oil fires continued to shock the area, however. The land and seas were still reeling from their oil bath. Many plants and animals were dead, and scientists believed that some turtle species might have been driven to extinction. People were healthy for the moment, but doctors worried that the future might produce cancer, birth defects, and other dire consequences of living amid the pollutants.

Area economies, particularly Kuwait's, were also in trouble. The costs sustained by the oil industry alone were staggering. The U.S. Department of Defense estimates that between lost production, spilled oil, well-control costs, and damaged well repair, the Gulf War and the oil fires that followed it had cost Kuwait $30 to $50 billion. The cost of destroyed crops and livestock is not known, but it surely was astronomical. Combined with war-related expenses that had nothing to do with the oil fires, these losses promised to burden Kuwait's economy for decades to come.

CHAPTER 5

Studying the Disaster

Before 1991, the world had never experienced an environmental catastrophe like the oil fires of Kuwait. Scientists therefore did not know what to expect. Would the oil fires cause a worldwide disaster, would their effects be strictly local, or would the answer lie somewhere between these extremes? Theories started flying during the early part of the Gulf War, when Iraq publicly threatened to destroy Kuwait's oil industry. After the oil wells ignited and the disaster became reality, scientists set to work proving—and disproving—these theories.

By 1997, the health and environmental consequences of the Gulf War had still not been adequately studied. Many soldiers, such as Sergeant First Class Carol Picou, pictured here holding a photograph of a bombing site in Kuwait, believe that ailments they have suffered since their tour are the result of poisons they were exposed to during the war. (Photo courtesy of Associated Press)

Dire Predictions

The first prediction of catastrophe came from Dr. Abdullah Toukan, science adviser to Jordan's King Hussein. In early January 1991, Toukan guessed that 500 oil wells might eventually go up in flames. He estimated that 3 million barrels of oil could spew from these wells each day. Toukan further calculated that in a year, this much burning oil could release 18.2 million tons (16.5 million mt) of soot into the air. If it rose high enough, the soot would escape from the *troposphere*, which starts at about 6 miles (9.6 km) above Earth's surface. The troposphere is the atmospheric layer in which clouds form. Rain and other natural forces would not be able to wash the high-flying soot back to the ground. The smoky debris would therefore travel around the world, blocking the Sun's rays and perhaps even changing Earth's climate. (The theory of why the soot would rise above the troposphere is detailed in the "Rising Soot" sidebar on this page.)

Toukan's predictions were based in part on the concept of *nuclear winter*. Scientists Carl Sagan, Paul Crutzen, and Richard Turco had introduced the nuclear winter theory in 1982. The theory addressed the possible results of a global nuclear war and the many fires that would rage in its aftermath. These fires would release pollutants and soot that would cause a worldwide darkening and cooling of the atmosphere. The effects would cause significant destruction to most species living on the planet. Toukan admitted that 500 oil fires would release only a tiny fraction of the soot needed to cause a theoretical

Rising Soot

The prediction that soot from Kuwait's oil fires would rise above the troposphere was based on a concept called *self-lofting*. This phrase means that the soot itself causes a series of reactions that lifts the soot higher and higher. Specifically, the dark soot absorbs heat from the Sun. The soot then releases some of this heat and warms up the surrounding air. Warm air rises. Scientists believed that the soot would catch a ride on this warm air, moving higher and higher until it left the "weather zone" of the troposphere. In the case of the Kuwaiti oil fires, self-lofting did not happen, mostly because the smoke was not as dark as scientists had expected it to be. The smoke therefore did not absorb enough heat to raise itself above the troposphere.

A thick, black cloud of smoke hangs over the skyline of Kuwait City in March 1991. On a typical day, the smoke would eventually disperse, making it seem as if the Sun were rising in the middle of the day. (Photo courtesy of Associated Press)

nuclear winter, but he also felt that the threat to the world was so serious that it could not be ignored.

Toukan's comments were soon backed up by one of the scientists who had created the nuclear winter theory in the first place. On January 22, Dr. Carl Sagan aired his views on the television news program *Nightline*:

> We think the net effects [of the oil fires] will be very similar to the explosion of the Indonesian volcano Tambora in 1815, which resulted in the year 1816 being known as the year without a summer. There were massive agricultural failures in North America and in western Europe, and very serious human suffering, and in

some cases starvation. Especially for South Asia, that seems to be in the cards, and perhaps for a significant fraction of the Northern Hemisphere as well.

Some scientists, including nuclear winter theorist Richard Turco, later tried to soften Sagan's words. "Comparisons with nuclear winter [are] irrelevant," Dr. Turco said. He also suggested that Sagan's comments had been taken out of context: "[TV] is a sound-bite environment, and you do the best you can. But it seems as if all the contingencies get dropped out, and you get saddled with one prediction, and it's hard to back out." Still, the prediction had been made. Alarmed by Sagan's words, the world scientific community prepared to study a disaster of epic proportions.

Flying through the Fog

There was little that researchers could do in the early months of the oil fires. The governments of Kuwait and nearby countries were busy with war-related matters, and scientific research was not considered a priority. By mid-May, however, research teams began to arrive on the scene. They hoped to study the black plume rising from Kuwait's blazing oil fields and find out exactly how damaging it really was.

The earliest studies were done by the U.S. National Center for Atmospheric Research (NCAR) and the University of Washington in Seattle. Every day, scientists from these organizations flew back and forth through the plume in airplanes filled with special smoke-monitoring equipment. Study teams would eventually log more than 200 hours of flight time. During these flights, they covered the entire gulf coast and gathered massive amounts of data. Because the position of the plume changed constantly, scientists did not know where they would be flying each day. They studied satellite pictures each morning to see where the plume was blowing and then planned their day's activities accordingly.

Others soon joined the first two teams. Researchers arrived from Britain, Germany, and other countries to take additional measurements. Airplanes within the plume took some of these measurements; other measurements were taken on the ground. All of the information was combined to create one source called the Kuwait Data Archive.

Before they studied the data that they had gathered, scientists feared the worst. Conditions within the plume were dreadful. In a 2001 interview, NCAR scientist Lawrence Radke remembered one flight in particular. "Suddenly the lights went out as we got thick into the plume," he said. "Something like less than one percent of the visible radiation from the sun was reaching us. It was black inside the airplane." Scientist Bruce Morley added his perspective: "Sitting in the back of the airplane, I couldn't see anything. It just got black in the airplane and it happened very quickly." Researchers wore gas masks to protect themselves from sulfur dioxide and other pollutants that were thick enough to cause throat irritation and coughing. Oily soot outside the planes covered everything with greasy streaks and smears. "The airplane came back blacker every day," recalled Radke.

Surprising Results

Data analysis showed that the situation was not as bad as scientists had feared. Within the plume, levels of dangerous gases such as sulfur dioxide, hydrogen sulfide, carbon monoxide, and nitrogen oxides were much lower than expected. The oil fires seemed to be burning more efficiently than scientists had imagined they would. They were gobbling up most of the poisonous gases before the gases could escape into the air.

Soot levels were also surprisingly low compared to early predictions. NCAR scientists reported that the oil fires would pump about 1.37 million tons (1.24 million mt) of soot into the air over the course of a year—*if* the fires continued to burn at their peak

After the Persian Gulf War, soot from the oil well fires could be seen from space. This photograph was taken from the space shuttle Atlantis *in March 1991. (Digital image 1996 CORBIS; original photo courtesy of NASA/CORBIS)*

rate. This figure was much lower than Toukan's estimate of 18.2 million tons (16.5 million mt)—and even this modest figure was unrealistically high, since well-control specialists were putting out more fires every day. As the fires died down, so did the amount of soot being released.

NCAR scientists also discovered that the soot was not rising as high as Toukan and others had predicted. The top of the plume usually hovered between 10,000 and 16,000 feet (3,050 and 4,880 m). Occasionally it rose to 20,000 feet (6,100 m), but even this was not

nearly high enough for the smoke to leave the troposphere. The oily particles rising from Kuwait's burning wells remained stuck in the cloud zone, where they would eventually be captured by raindrops and then washed from the air during storms.

This "washing out" effect itself was another surprising finding. Scientists originally thought that because oil and water do not mix well, raindrops would not absorb smoke from an oil fire. Therefore, the smoke would stay in the air for a long time and travel far from its source. This theory turned out to be wrong. Oily soot contains a lot of sulfate, a chemical that is attracted to water. Researchers discovered that contrary to all expectations, Kuwait's smoke plume was very easily flushed from the skies by Earth's natural weather processes.

Flight teams were not the only ones to discover better-than-expected conditions in and around Kuwait. The U.S. Environmental Protection Agency (EPA) and other organizations that took measurements at ground level reported very similar results. According to multiple studies, the amounts of sulfur dioxide, nitrogen oxides, carbon monoxide, and ozone in the air were no worse than one might expect to find in an urban area like Los Angeles, California. Medical studies, though limited in scope, seemed to back up this finding. For example, Dr. Mostafa Desouky, who monitored air quality for Kuwait's Environmental Protection Agency, said in a 1991 interview, "We didn't find any difference before and after the well fires for the prevalence of chest complaints."

International Outcry

Most scientists accepted the results from NCAR and other agencies without question, but a few people were outraged. Officials from Friends of the Earth publicly announced their disgust. "[The EPA report] read as if they'd visited a neighborhood bonfire to toast some marshmallows," complained Brent Blackwelder.

Officials from the environmental organization Greenpeace also objected to the rosy picture being painted in Kuwait. They pointed out that pollutant levels changed from day to day, ranging from light to horrible. Averaging methods, they said, hid the pollution "spikes" and made conditions seem better than they really were. Greenpeace and other organizations also commented that most studies looked only for certain pollutants. Trace amounts of other dangerous substances might be floating in Kuwait's air, but without proper analysis, people would never know about these materials. Tony Horwitz, a reporter covering the crisis for the *Wall Street Journal,* said that "when we started hearing official statements that (the pollution) wasn't so dangerous, it really went against the evidence of the eyes."

Critics felt that politicians were influencing the studies being done in Kuwait. Some people claimed that the U.S. government did not want any bad news to weaken its victory in the Gulf War. Others thought that the U.S. government was trying to dodge future health insurance claims by Gulf War veterans. The Kuwaiti government

A former soldier in the Gulf War, Brian Martin suffers from many ailments that he attributes to breathing many toxic substances during his time in Kuwait. In this 1996 photograph, he is pictured with the cane he uses to help him walk. (Photo courtesy of Associated Press)

was also seen as having a political agenda. "[Officials] refused to tell the people that the air might be dangerous, because they said that if they did, people would panic and not work to rebuild the country," said Dr. Sami al-Yakoob of the Kuwait Institute of Scientific Research (KISR). The Kuwaiti public was skeptical about the government's attitude. "How could you believe it [the Kuwaiti government] when you had those scientists from the university and [KISR] saying that it might be dangerous, and when you looked all around you and saw that the air was black?" asked one citizen.

Despite the outcry, scientists who were involved in the studies did not budge from their position. Lawrence Radke insisted that "nothing we saw in the chemistry…would suggest a big health problem at the surface." Scientist Darrel Baumgardner agreed:

> There were some problems near the fires on the ground. But downwind—I have never seen anything published that showed that there was any major problem from the smoke….
>
> I read several articles that stated we were withholding some of the data…. As far as I know, there was certainly no cover-up….
>
> The archive was open and we handed out the data freely. We had some orientation on how to handle the press, and we basically said, "No. This is all open. We're not going to hide anything here; there's nothing to hide."

Questions Remain

As far as most scientists were concerned, only one real health question remained after the studies in Kuwait were completed. Researchers were not able to figure out whether Kuwait's oil fires were exposing people to more airborne particles than usual. Typical air particle pollution comes from fuel burning, industrial processes, transportation, and even dusty roads. Most air particles

Missing Data

Although researchers found reassuringly low levels of air pollution while Kuwait's oil fires burned, they were missing one important piece of information. They did not have the equipment to measure airborne particles less than 10 microns (0.00003 inches) in length. (A *micron* is one-thousandth of a millimeter.) Particles of this size can be breathed deep into human lungs, where they can do damage over time. Burning tends to create a great deal of such particles. Some researchers worry that the oil fires may have dumped large amounts of these invisible poisons into Kuwait's air.

are too big to get past the filters in human air passages to do internal damage. But when particles of a certain size are able to enter the lungs and bloodstream, serious damage can occur. Most common ailments caused by airborne particle pollution include irritation of eyes, throat, or lungs. If Kuwait's residents were breathing too many tiny particles, they might have long-term lung scarring later. The particles might also be carrying poisonous chemicals released by the oil burning. When these pollutants seep into people's bodies, they can eventually cause cancer.

Measurements taken at ground level did show a very high level of particles in the air, but it was hard to learn the reason for these readings. Even during normal times, Kuwait is one of the dustiest places on Earth, and the country always has a high air-particle count. Also, because tanks had torn up Kuwait's desert surface during the Gulf War, spring windstorms kicked up more sand and dust than usual in 1991. Therefore, although everyone agreed that particle counts were high, it was hard to tell exactly how much of the problem was caused by the oil fires. (Research on the air pollution may have been incomplete, as told in the "Missing Data" sidebar on this page.)

Another lingering question involved the oil fires' effects on world climate. Some scientists thought that Kuwait's oily smoke might have contributed to unusually bad spring weather in Bangladesh and India, and astronauts reported that Earth's atmosphere looked smokier than usual from space. However, the general feeling was that the oil fires did not cause these effects. Most researchers agreed that although the fires caused temporary changes to local climates, they did not have much—if any—

The Pinatubo Problem

The worldwide effects of the Kuwaiti oil fires may have been masked by the eruption of Mount Pinatubo, a large volcano in the Philippines. This volcano burst into life in June 1991, belching more than 20 million tons (18 million mt) of dust and ash into the atmosphere. Pinatubo's smoke rose more than 20 miles (32 km) above Earth's surface and then traveled around the world. Temperature measurements by satellites showed that this smoke blocked some of the Sun's rays and lowered average global temperatures by about 1 °F (0.6 °C). Any widespread effects of the Kuwaiti oil fires would have been dwarfed by this natural disaster.

global effect. (One reason why worldwide effects of the disaster may not have seemed so bad is given in "The Pinatubo Problem" sidebar above.)

The Scope of the Disaster

All in all, the findings of the many studies of Kuwait were surprisingly positive. The results showed that the frightening nuclear winter theory was exaggerated; the effects of the smoke on worldwide climate were limited or nonexistent; and the impacts of the smoke plume on human health, while still uncertain, did not seem to be disastrous. (More about the fires' effects on health can be found in Chapter 6.) The global situation was better than anyone had dared to expect.

In a local sense, though, the picture was not so positive. No one could deny that the oil fires had been devastating to the residents, economies, and environments of some Middle Eastern nations. To the people who had to rebuild their shattered countries and lives in the aftermath of the Kuwaiti oil fires, the scientists' optimistic findings were small consolation, indeed.

CHAPTER 6

Long-Term Effects

This February 1991 photograph shows a boom working to contain oil along the coast of Saudi Arabia. In an attempt to hold back U.S. troops, Iraqi soldiers dumped great quantities of oil into the gulf that traveled from Kuwait City south to Saudi Arabia. (Photo courtesy of Greg E. Mathieson/MAI/Landov)

From the day that Kuwait's oil fires ignited, scientists were sure that the fires would have long-term effects on the region's people and environment, but no one knew exactly what these effects would be. Despite many predictions, it was understood that only time, attention, and careful research would reveal the truth.

Scientists know more about the impact of the Kuwaiti oil fires today, more than a decade after the last blaze was extinguished. Some information has come from experiments and studies. Scientists gained other information by simply watching and waiting. One by one, the questions raised in 1991 are being answered in the shifting of Kuwait's waters and sands.

Health Effects

The most confusing issue to arise during the fires was the possible long-term health effects of oil and smoke exposure. Would residents of Kuwait and other smoky areas suffer from higher-than-usual rates of cancer, birth defects, and other serious health conditions? The answer to this question still is not clear, and it probably never will be. To understand whether things have changed since the Gulf War, researchers would need accurate statistics about the population's health *before* the war. Such statistics do not exist. Researchers also could not study people at the height of the oil fires, because of wartime conditions. This information would have been very important in setting up long-term comparison studies. The population of Kuwait also shifted dramatically during the postwar years. Many people relocated, fearing for their health or coping with the loss of business due to the depressed economy. New people moved to Kuwait in the years after the war and subsequent cleanup, so health comparisons are virtually useless.

Some general information was gathered in the years following the fires. Samples of Kuwait's smoky air had been collected during 1991. These samples were later analyzed to see if they contained dangerous levels of metals, chemicals, and gases. In general, they did not. Every now and then, a single pollutant might spike at a high level, but these spikes did not last long. On most days, the air quality fell within ranges considered safe. In the words of the U.S. National Defense Research Institute, the "concentrations of the pollutants measured in the Gulf…were lower than those in U.S. urban areas. Thus, one would not expect [the] population to experience ill health effects as a result of exposures in the Gulf." Furthermore, "no evidence of health effects…[was] found in the peer-reviewed literature."

A study of wildcats seemed to support this view. Researchers gathered 26 smoke-exposed cats from Ahmadi, where many of

Gulf War veteran Floyd McCain displays photographs of lesions on his arms and legs. McCain, who went to the gulf with the 1208th Quartermaster Corps of the U.S. Army, claims that he has endured skin cancer, headaches, dizziness, and loss of memory as a result of poisons ingested during his time in Kuwait. He is one of many soldiers who are interested in continuing research on the health effects of the 1991 Gulf War. (Photo courtesy of Associated Press)

the burning oil fields were located, and nearby Kuwait City. The cats' lungs, livers, and kidneys were examined, and urine and blood samples were analyzed. The researchers concluded that the cats did not show any symptoms of long-term harm.

Another study examined birth defects among children of Gulf War veterans. Between 1991 and 1993, babies born to U.S. soldiers who had served in the war did not have an unusually high level of birth defects. In fact, their level of birth defects was slightly *lower* than normal. Other studies, including some done in Kuwaiti hospitals, found similar results.

Basing their conclusions on studies like these, most U.S. scientists believe today that the oil fires did not do lasting damage to human health, but doctors in Kuwait tend to disagree. In a 1996 survey, almost all of the doctors questioned believed that respiratory diseases had increased since the Gulf War. More than half thought that oil fire pollution had increased the rate of miscarriage, and more than two-thirds believed that there was a strong relationship between lung disease and oil fire smoke. But it is important to note that these findings are based on opinion only and are not backed up by any scientific data.

Another area of debate involves Gulf War syndrome, a mysterious illness that is said to have affected thousands of soldiers who spent time in Kuwait during the war. No one is sure what causes the syndrome, but according to some scientists, the soldiers' symptoms point to smoke and oil exposure. One researcher said,

> Studies of professional firefighters in the U.S. have found smoke exposure leads to asthma, respiratory disease, and lung impairment. Occupational and animal studies of petroleum inhalation and skin exposure have found symptoms that include cancer, fatigue, asthma, breathlessness, headache, skin rash, immune suppression, memory loss and chemical sensitivity. All these symptoms have been found among the ill Gulf War veterans.

Is there a link between these chronic health ailments and the exposure to pollutants that the soldiers faced in Kuwait? All U.S. government agencies, including the Department of Veterans Affairs, say that there is not. A study by the independent agency Green Cross International mentioned many possible causes of Gulf War syndrome but did not include oil and smoke exposure on this list. Still, some people will always believe that the Kuwaiti oil fires played a key role in this disease. These critics feel that the government is hiding information regarding Gulf War syndrome, but without hard evidence, the truth will never be known.

Oily Soil

The long-term effects of the oil fires on Kuwait's land are much easier to measure. In early 1992, satellite pictures showed that about 700 square miles (1,810 km²) of desert (approximately 10 percent of Kuwait's land area) was blanketed with oil lakes, tar mats, or soot. By 1995, just three years later, that figure had dropped to about 150 square miles (390 km²). Oil lakes accounted for only about 15 square miles (39 km²), or 10 percent of this area.

The satellite pictures do not tell the whole story. "In most places, the soot...remained...concealed under a veneer of sand [which] was why [it was] not observed on the satellite image," said one researcher. In a 1998 report, Green Cross International commented that oil sludge in the remaining lakes had sunk several feet into the soil. "One needs only to scratch the desert to find the remains of the continuing environmental damage," this report stated. "There are many areas where oiled sand...lies at the surface or just below, and these areas clearly show no or reduced amounts of vegetation." In severely polluted areas, these conditions will probably persist for decades, or perhaps centuries.

All the news from Kuwait's deserts is not bad. Scientists have been pleasantly surprised to discover that many areas recovered more quickly than expected. By the spring of 1995, for instance, many badly oiled areas were covered with blooming wildflowers. This was partly because of a chemical balancing effect. Alkaline soot and carbon from the oil fires neutralized Kuwait's naturally acidic deserts, making it easier for certain plants to grow. Researchers also found that oil-eating bacteria had started to grow among plants' roots, protecting them from the polluted soil. "We think that God has laid in nature a huge amount of resilience that you cannot destroy easily," marveled one Kuwaiti scientist.

Polluted Groundwater

Although Kuwait's plants will recover over time, scientists worry that the country's water supplies may not. Kuwait has just two natural freshwater reservoirs—one at Um Al-Aish and one at Raudhatain. In 1998 studies showed that oil had seeped into the Um Al-Aish reservoir. As a result, all wells in the area had to be closed. Then in 2002, KISR completed a study showing that the Raudhatain reservoir had also become polluted.

The loss of these water sources was a blow to Kuwait's security. Together, Um Al-Aish and Raudhatain were the nation's only backup water supplies in case desalination plants or other freshwater sources failed. To fix the problem, Kuwait proposes to pump contaminated water from the ground, treat it, and then return it to the ground. The country also proposes to clean oil-contaminated soil above and around the reservoirs, but doing so

Pollution from the Gulf War has tainted Kuwait's ocean water and its supply of fresh water. (Photo courtesy of CORBIS/SYGMA)

Kuwaiti government official Abdullah Kubeshi collects a sample of crude oil from an oil lake formed in 1991 after the Iraqi army set over 700 wells on fire at the nearby Burgan oil field. Almost a decade later, some of the oil has seeped so deeply into the desert that it will never be recovered. (Photo courtesy of Associated Press)

is a huge undertaking. "At least ten million cubic meters [353 million cubic feet] of oil-contaminated soil must be [cleaned]," said Green Cross International. Furthermore, "the heavily contaminated sand must be viewed as a toxic waste and solutions must be found for its temporary safe storage." The effort will be expensive and difficult, but if the work is not done soon, scientists fear that oil will sink so deep into Kuwait's deserts that it may never be recovered.

Some scientists, in fact, think that it may already be too late. Researcher and environmentalist Jean-Michel Cousteau claims that "there is at present no technological fix for this problem." Documentary filmmaker Paula DiPerna agrees: "Once ground water [sic] is contaminated, it's virtually impossible to clean it up. So [Kuwait's freshwater supplies] will probably never be cleaned up." If these observers are right, tainted water may turn out to be one of the oil fires' longest-lasting impacts.

The State of the Sea

The health of the Persian Gulf is the last major area of environmental concern (for reasons detailed in the "A Vital Resource" sidebar on the following page). In this area, much of the news is good. Constant water movement tends to clean oceans fairly quickly, and the Persian Gulf has turned out to be no exception. Because the gulf has a narrow entrance and does not mingle freely with larger water bodies, recovery has taken a bit longer than it might have in another area. Nonetheless, Green Cross International found that the gulf environment was fairly healthy by 1998. Coral reefs, which are especially fragile, did not show major damage from their oil bath. Some sea animals, including shrimp and fish, were found to have oil-contaminated flesh, but the contamination levels were very low, and the populations of these animals were strong overall.

A Vital Resource

Why is the health of the Persian Gulf so important? A 1992 Greenpeace report summed it up with these words.

The Gulf is one of the most productive water bodies in the world.... A healthy Gulf is fundamental to the survival of the region and its environment—which includes the people. The sea provides fresh water via desalination plants; fisheries are a multi-million dollar industry and wildlife includes birds (between one and two million wintering birds per year), turtles (Green and Hawksbill—both endangered) and various marine mammals including rare dolphins and the dugong. The ecosystems—seagrasses, coral reefs, intertidal mudflats and mangroves, on which these and other species depend—are vital, but fragile. During the war there were warnings that great ecological damage would result if large concentrations of oil reached these sensitive habitats.

Beaches along the Persian Gulf coast were more of a concern. Both visible and underground oil still polluted beaches in southern Kuwait and northern Saudi Arabia years after the war. Scientists worried that this oil would damage plant and animal life as it seeped slowly into the environment. Some environmentalists continued to call for a cleanup, but others believed that it was better to let nature take its course. Oil is a natural substance, and it does break down over time without human help. There is even some evidence that seaside areas recover more quickly from oil spills if people stay out of the way. In the gulf's case, it seems that this natural recovery is well under way.

Major cleanup efforts in the gulf seem especially discouraging for another reason. The Persian Gulf is the world's oil tanker superhighway, and as such, it may be the planet's most polluted sea. An estimated 250,000 barrels of oil escape from ships into the gulf each year. This is about the same amount of oil that was lost in the 1989 *Exxon Valdez* disaster in Alaska's Prince William Sound, which attracted worldwide attention. But in the gulf, this level of pollution is acceptable. The oil in the water is considered one of the costs of doing business. In the long term, the damage done when the Iraqis dumped Kuwaiti oil into the gulf may be minor compared to the steady seepage from the country's healthy oil industry.

CHAPTER 7

The Economic Damage

In March 2003, the impending crisis in Iraq worried officials at Kuwait Oil Company's Gas Operations. In this photograph, workers adjust one of the flowlines at the Maqwa oil field, south of Kuwait City, and ready their oil supplies in case of war. (Photo courtesy of Associated Press)

Environmental damage was the most talked-about aspect of the Kuwaiti oil fires disaster. The effects of the fires on land, sea, and people were so dramatic that they understandably took center stage in the months and years following the Gulf War. However, the fires also caused another, less publicized problem: They had a huge effect on Kuwait's economy and industries.

Kuwait's Oil Industry

The well fires hit Kuwait's oil and petroleum industry hardest. Before the war, the KOC operated 944 oil wells. Together these wells produced up to 3 million barrels of oil per day. Selling at about $19 per barrel in 1990, this oil represented an income of roughly $28.5 million per day. In addition to its oil wells, the KOC also operated many support facilities. The company had 26 gathering centers that collected crude oil. The KOC also had many tanks where the oil was temporarily stored and had four terminals where oil was prepared for export and loaded onto ships and trucks. The company also operated a huge network of pipelines that carried oil between these facilities.

Most of the KOC's equipment was severely damaged by the Gulf War. In late February 1991, 788 of the KOC's wells were on fire, gushing oil, or otherwise damaged. Eight of the company's gathering stations had been destroyed, and the rest were unusable. Holding tanks were cracked, pipelines were broken, and all four of the country's oil terminals were badly damaged. As a result of all this destruction, Kuwait's petroleum industry crashed to a halt.

The lack of oil production was not the only issue facing the KOC. At the height of the oil fires, an estimated 11 million barrels of oil were escaping each day from damaged wellheads. This oil was burning up in the fires and flowing onto the land and into the sea. Some of the pooling oil would be recovered, but much would not—and the burning oil, of course, was gone for good. Billions of dollars in future income were disappearing into the air and seas, never to be restored.

The recovery from the oil fires was achieved in two phases. The KOC named the first phase Al-Awda, meaning "the return." The main goals of Al-Awda were putting out the oil fires and capping damaged wells. This phase was completed on November 6, 1991, when the last burning well was extinguished. (Al-Awda's accomplishments are highlighted in the "Al-Awda's Achievements" sidebar below.) The KOC then moved on to Al-Tameer, or "the reconstruction." During this phase, the company focused on recovering and treating oil from the many lakes dotting the country. The KOC also worked to fix wells, gathering centers, storage tanks, and export facilities.

The main focus of Al-Tameer was to restore oil production to prewar levels. In this respect, the operation was a huge success. The KOC had originally hoped to produce 1.5 million barrels of oil per day by March 1993. The company reached this production goal in October 1992—five months ahead of schedule. By February 1993, oil output had reached 2 million barrels per day, where it leveled out and remained. The industry had recovered years earlier than expected. In the short term, the episode did cost

Al-Awda's Achievements

Al-Awda accomplished many important tasks, including the following:

- 751 damaged wells extinguished and controlled

- 647 burning or gushing wells controlled

- More than 245 miles (394 km) of flowlines laid

- 174 miles (280 km) of special access roads constructed

- 353 water lagoons excavated, lined, and filled

- More than 20,000 items of unexploded ordnance destroyed

- More than 3,000 telephones procured and installed

- More than 3.5 million meals prepared

Al-Awda was successful, but more work remains if Kuwait's landscape is ever to recover fully.

the KOC an astronomical amount (estimates place the cost between $30 billion and $50 billion). But apart from lost oil reserves, it is fair to say that the Kuwaiti oil fires disaster did very little long-term harm to the country's oil industry.

Agriculture

The same seems to be true of agriculture. Farming is of little importance to Kuwait's economy, since only about 1 percent of the land is under cultivation, due to the hot, dry weather and lack of irrigation water. The country's small agricultural industries, including greenhouses, livestock farms, and poultry farms, were largely destroyed by the oil fires and other effects of the Gulf War.

By 1998, greenhouses and farms had been restored. Chickens were once again laying eggs, and livestock was able to graze again in most parts of the desert. In a few former grazing areas, salt water had been used by firefighters. The salt water sank into the soil and changed its chemistry. Because plants that used to thrive in these areas cannot grow in the salty ground, they have not returned, but salt-tolerant plants have replaced them. Grazing livestock will not eat the new plants, so these once valuable areas are now useless to farmers. Little is being done to remedy this situation.

Some scientists are concerned that oil remaining in the desert may affect agriculture in the future. They think that oil products could enter the grasses and plants eaten by livestock. The animals that eat these plants might get sick, or they might store the dangerous chemicals in their flesh. Humans who eat the meat of these animals might ingest the contaminants and get sick themselves. Milk, eggs, and other products from contaminated animals could also be dangerous. Long-term monitoring is needed to make sure such problems do not arise.

Contaminated irrigation water is another concern. Kuwait collects and uses its brackish (undrinkable) groundwater for farming. So far, there are no signs that this water is tainted with

Camels graze on a farm near Jahara, Kuwait. Although agriculture accounts for only a small part of Kuwait's economy, some of the country's nomadic people have been forced to look elsewhere for grazing regions within Kuwait as a result of poisoned land. (Photo courtesy of Associated Press)

oil or other pollutants, but it could become contaminated as the spilled oil beneath Kuwait's sands continues to sink and spread. If this water was then used to water crops, it could harm both the plants and the people and animals that eat them. Careful monitoring is necessary to prevent both a health crisis and economic disaster.

Fisheries

Fish from the Persian Gulf, such as barracuda, king mackerel, and local fish called *subaitee* and *hamour,* as well as shrimp, are important food and income sources for Kuwait. These populations were badly hurt by the oil fires and slicks of the Gulf War. Many animals died of oil poisoning. Others survived the oil but later died because of changes in the gulf's ecology. For instance, the smoke plume hovering above the gulf blocked sunlight for months on end, thereby changing the water's temperature. This prevented some creatures from reproducing or hatching from their eggs, in turn affecting other animals higher up the food chain. Oil and oily fallout from the fires also destroyed some creatures' habitats, causing these animals to move away or die out.

These impacts were felt strongly when the war first ended. The shrimp industry in particular seemed to be in big trouble: The 1991–1992 shrimping season had to be closed early because there were so few shrimp to catch. Fishing boats reported better catches than shrimp boats, but fishermen did notice a change in the types of fish that they were catching. They worried that some species might have been permanently reduced. They also worried that fish populations might drop over time. Fish live longer than shrimp, so if they are not reproducing, it takes much longer for a problem to appear.

By 1998, Kuwait's fisheries seemed to be out of danger. Catch rates for both shrimp and fish were about the same as prewar levels, suggesting that populations had recovered from the events of 1991. Some scientists continued to worry that oil pollution near the Kuwaiti and Saudi shorelines might hurt these animals in the future, but according to Green Cross International, "there is no evidence that [war] impacts should alter these parameters seven years later." Important commercial species seemed likely to recover fully from the events of the war, and so did the industries that depended on these animals.

In one indirect way, the oil fires are still hurting Kuwait's fishing operations. Fishermen who made no money during the Gulf War were in bad financial shape after the war ended. During the postwar years, they caught many more shrimp and fish than usual to make up for their lost income. This put a strain on the gulf's resources that continues to this day. In fact, said Green Cross International, "The increase in fishing pressure…[has] had and should continue to have more detrimental effects on the biological [resources] than the oil pollution itself."

Iraq Must Pay

This photograph, taken in March 1991, shows a decimated convoy of Iraqi vehicles. Iraqi forces attempting to flee Kuwait were defeated by coalition soldiers. (Photo courtesy of Associated Press)

Iraq directly caused most of Kuwait's oil fires, so it received little sympathy in the world press after the Gulf War. It is important to mention, however, that this country also suffered economically from the oil fires and their aftermath. The global community feels that Iraq and its leader at the time, Saddam Hussein, should be held accountable for the damage they caused. As a result of the U.S. invasion of Iraq in 2003 and Hussein's subsequent capture, it seems likely that he will finally have to answer for his actions.

To determine the cost of the damage, the UN in 1991 formed the United Nations Compensation Commission (UNCC). The purpose of the UNCC is to collect and evaluate claims from countries that feel that they have been financially harmed by the Gulf War. The deadline for all claims was February 1, 1997. By the time that this deadline arrived, nearly 100 governments had submitted a total of 2.6 million claims. Added up, these claims asked for about $350 billion in damages from Iraq. Environmental claims made up about $80 billion of this figure.

Not all of these claims would be granted. The UNCC estimated that only 18 percent of the claims against Iraq would ultimately succeed. Still, this left Iraq responsible for tens of billions of dollars in repayment. The money was to come from the country's oil sales, which are monitored carefully by the international community. A percentage of every sale went into a UN account that was used to repay war victims.

Although this plan was considered viable at the time, it has become clear that few dollars have been repaid to Kuwait. Iraq was torn apart by the first Gulf War. The government badly needed money to rebuild its hospitals, roads, utilities, and other facilities, and hundreds of thousands of citizens who were not responsible for their leaders' choices were plunged into sickness, poverty, and starvation. Partly because Iraq's income was being tapped by the UNCC, the money to fix these problems was not available, and the rest of the world, angered by Iraq's actions during the Gulf War, was not particularly quick to provide aid.

Additionally, corruption at the highest levels of Iraq's government resulted in oil revenues being siphoned into the personal accounts of the nation's leaders. With Iraq now in the throes of rebuilding itself after the 2003 invasion by the United States, it is still uncertain what money can be directed to repay Kuwait in the future.

CHAPTER 8

After the Fires

Kuwait City has largely recovered from the disaster of the oil fire crisis. The harbor is again a place of beauty where residents and tourist alike spend leisure time. Large deposits of soot and oil still remain, however, in the desert. (Photo courtesy of Associated Press)

A visitor to Kuwait City today would find little evidence of the oil fires that raged not long ago. The city's downtown area has been cleaned up, and damaged buildings have been fixed. Private homes also are in good shape, and new mansions are sprouting up all around the city. Expensive cars jam the country's streets, all of which have been repaired and show no signs of war damage.

The country's ruler, Emir Jaber al-Ahmad al-Jaber al-Sabah, is the proud resident of a brand-new $500 million palace. "Present-day Kuwait shows no physical signs of the arson and vandalism the Iraqis left in their wake…. Everything gleams as it did before," reported the August 2003 issue of *Kuwait News*. (One edifice, however, is not the same as it was before the war, as detailed in the "History Erased" sidebar on this page.)

The country's population is now back to normal. Many low-income workers from India, the Philippines, and other poor nations fled from Kuwait during the Gulf War and its aftermath. These workers made up more than half of Kuwait's prewar population. Their departure left no one to handle waste removal, farming, and many of the country's other day-to-day functions. The workers have now returned—and they have brought Kuwait's former vitality with them. In both looks and function, Kuwait's cities have recovered from the 1991 oil fires disaster.

History Erased

Kuwait's former national museum is a sad reminder of the Gulf War. The museum was once full of treasures and artifacts, but it was looted and then set on fire by Iraqi soldiers during the 1991 conflict. Only a few exhibits have been recovered, and today, most of the museum stands as an empty shell.

Scars Remain

Outside the cities, scars linger. From the air, it is easy to see the large patches of soot and tar that still coat the desert in some places. *Oil trenches* (deep cuts made to channel oil pools at the height of the fires) crisscross the land. Most of the oil pools themselves have dried up or sunk into the sand, but a few remain. They are sticky and thick from years of evaporation, and they will be difficult or impossible to clean up.

Amid the damage, the KOC's equipment stands out. Nearly all the oil wells, tanks, and other necessities have been fixed or replaced. But one corner of the Burgan oil field is filled with blackened and twisted equipment. Steel girders droop; partly melted water tanks slump to the ground. A crusty coating of oil blankets everything. "We saved this so people could see it," explained KOC public relations officer Mutlaq al-Qahtani. "It's a site of international robbery."

Less visible is damage to the desert surface. During the war, tanks and other vehicles tore up the hardened top layer of sand. After the war, heavy equipment used by firefighting crews did the same thing. As a result, many sandy areas are much looser than they used to be. Because loose sand can be picked up and carried by the wind, sandstorms in Kuwait have been unusually intense since the war. There is no telling when—or indeed, if—this situation will change.

The desert was not the only landform that was a victim of the war. The beaches of Kuwait and Saudi Arabia also bear the lasting marks of the oil fires. Oily coatings still cover the shore and seabed in some places. In other places, the oil is not visible, because it has been buried under fresh sand, but digging down just a few inches reveals the tarry truth below. "It's going to take years and maybe generations to remove these marks," said Dr. Samira Omar of KISR. "These are deep, deep scars in the environment."

Cleanup Efforts

Judging by current efforts, it is likely that Kuwait's pollution problems will continue for a long time. Very little environmental work has been done since the days immediately following the Gulf War, when recovering spilled oil was an economic priority for the KOC. At that time, the oil was reasonably fresh, so it could be refined and sold. Now, cleaning up is only an expense, not an opportunity to make money, so no one is doing it on a large scale. This situation angers people who feel that the Kuwaiti government should be taking a more active role. "We are a rich country and can afford to pay for cleanup. But we will have these problems until someone from the government says, 'Give us all the experts

in the world to fix it,'" griped one environmental activist. This person pointed out that even scientific study is being neglected: "There have not been any honest or sincere pollution studies since liberation [when coalition forces drove Iraqi forces from Kuwait], not from the Ministry of Health or Environment or the government."

There are some signs that the situation may be improving. In 1996 Kuwait established the Environment Public Authority to create and monitor environmental laws for the country. This organization may encourage future cleanup efforts. The UNCC also recently awarded Kuwait $108 million to fund a three- to five-year study of the environment. Perhaps this study will reveal ways to mend the damaged earth.

Some researchers are already trying one method of handling the remaining oil. The technique is called *bioremediation*, and it involves natural bacteria. When released into contaminated soil or sand, these bacteria turn oil into materials that act like fertilizers,

Many scientists in Kuwait and around the world would like to see pollution studies done on the air and land in and around Kuwait. Few believe that pollution from the oil well fires (like the one seen in this photograph) has not had some lasting effect on the environment. (Photo courtesy of REUTERS/CORBIS)

thus allowing plants to grow again. The Soil Bio-Remediated Park in Ahmadi is the showcase for this technology. Completed in 2000, the park bursts with bougainvillea, bottlebrush trees, saltbushes, wildflowers, and desert grasses—all planted in oil-blackened soil. Some scientists think that the Ahmadi experiment proves that bioremediation can play an important role in cleaning up Kuwait's deserts. KISR and the Arab Oil Company are now trying to figure out ways that bacteria can be used to break up Kuwait's remaining oil lakes.

The Kuwaiti government did not consider environmental damages as important as economic ones in the aftermath of the oil fire crisis. As a result, the shorebird population greatly suffered, and inadequate follow-up research has caused confusion about how far the wildlife community has rebounded in the last decade. (Photo courtesy of CORBIS/SYGMA)

An Uneasy Peace

Although Kuwait is recovering from its environmental damage, the country's emotional scars will take much longer to fade. One Kuwaiti writer describes Iraq's invasion as "a unilateral act of aggression, and a complete betrayal of the trust the Kuwaiti people had put in their northern neighbors." The destruction of the nation's oil industry, and the fires that followed, only increased the feeling of betrayal.

Long after the war, Kuwait continued to reel from the blow. When asked in 2000 if he still felt threatened by Iraq, Kuwait's defense minister responded emphatically. "Yes we do, yes we do, yes we do," said Sheikh Salem al-Sabah. "It is built in their mind and their thoughts that Kuwait is a part of Iraq. They will keep threatening Kuwaiti security." This attitude drove a massive military buildup in Kuwait. The country is estimated to have spent $12 billion on defense in the decade following the Gulf War—at least six times the amount that the KOC spent on environmental recovery.

Kuwait's fears seemed to have been justified in early 2003. On the eve of war with the United States, Iraqi ruler Saddam Hussein once again threatened to flood the Middle East with oil. There were reports that Hussein had recruited terrorist groups to destroy oil facilities in Kuwait and Saudi Arabia. There were also rumors that Iraqi soldiers had been ordered to destroy oil wells in northern Iraq if war broke out.

U.S.-led forces invaded Iraq on March 20, 2003. Fearing another Kuwait situation, they moved quickly to take control of Iraq's oil industry. As a result, very little damage was done to the country's oil wells or other equipment.

Another worry eased on December 13, 2003, when Hussein was captured after a long search. Although responses to this news were mixed across the Middle East, as told in the "Mixed Reactions" sidebar on the following page, most Kuwaitis were

Mixed Reactions

The 2003 capture of Iraqi leader Saddam Hussein generated mixed reactions in the Arab world. Many people were unhappy: "It's bad news. To us, Saddam was a symbol of defiance to the U.S. plans in the region, and we support any person who stands in the face of American dominance," said one member of Jordan's parliament. "It's a black day in history," agreed a Palestinian citizen. "[Saddam] is the only man who said 'no' to American injustice in the Middle East."

In Kuwait, however, the primary reaction to Hussein's capture was joy. "We are so happy they got him," exclaimed one Kuwaiti. "Thank you, [U.S. president George W.] Bush. Thank you, U.S.A." Another resident agreed, explaining the national mood with these words: "Kuwait is unique among all these Arab countries because [people from other countries] don't know this man and they don't know Iraq. This has made the Kuwaiti people far happier than all people on Earth. Even the children are dancing."

happy that Hussein and his threats were gone for good. The future of Iraq-Kuwait relations was far from certain, but at least another oil fires disaster did not seem likely. In this respect, Kuwait—and the world—could finally breathe a sigh of relief.

CHAPTER 9

The Legacy of the Oil Fires

The Kuwaiti disaster was the worst series of oil fires ever to occur, and politically speaking, it was the most extreme act of ecological warfare that the world had ever seen. In both respects, the oil fires of 1991 were an invaluable learning experience for the world community.

U.S. Marines patrolled the edges of the burning oil fields in Kuwait in 1991. The soldiers' proximity to the poisonous soot, smoke, and gases emitted from the fires may be the reason that many have experienced sickness in the years following their time in the gulf region. (Photo courtesy of Associated Press)

Thanks to a favorable combination of climatic and geographic conditions, the Kuwaiti oil fires hurt few people directly. The flames could not travel across desert sands, so cities and homes did not burn. Also, smoke from the fires usually floated high above ground level, so most people in even the worst-affected areas could breathe without choking or suffocating. Several firefighters did lose their lives in oil field accidents, but these were isolated incidents. In general, Kuwait's human population weathered the disaster remarkably well.

Environmental Lessons

In the aftermath of the Gulf War, Kuwait's oil fires turned the Middle East into a gigantic natural laboratory. Before the fires, scientists had many theories about world climate; during the fires, they could actually test some of these theories under real conditions. They were surprised to find that many widely accepted ideas were false.

Earth, as it turns out, is not as easily harmed as people imagined it would be. Scientists had predicted severe problems resulting from climate change due to cooling from soot in the atmosphere. In reality, the soot never reached high enough to travel around the world and affect weather patterns. As the years pass, it is increasingly difficult to prove that environmental damage in Kuwait and beyond is due to the fires and not the general buildup of air pollution around the world. As one researcher pointed out, "Today's climate modelers obviously still have their limits. Now that the smoke is clearing, many people may wonder…if anyone should pay attention when they warn us of such other potential disasters as global warming." Do the results of the studies in Kuwait really apply so broadly? No true conclusions can be drawn with the information available today, but there is no doubt that an important question has been raised.

The world also learned a great deal from the local effects of the oil fires. Land, sea, animals, and people were damaged by smoke and oil from the blazes. To cope with this damage, researchers and rescuers had to develop new knowledge and techniques. Well-control specialists, for example, had to try many new firefighting methods before they figured out how to extinguish the worst of Kuwait's oil fires. Local rescue and relief organizations, put to the test for the first time, learned how to work efficiently during an emergency. Scientists were forced to develop new ways to clean oil-contaminated land and water. All this information will help people respond more effectively to future disasters around the world.

Cows grazing near oil fields set ablaze by Iraqis in 1991 run for cover away from the heat and smoke of the fires. (Photo courtesy of REUTERS/CORBIS)

Ongoing Worries

Human health continues to be an area of concern in and around Kuwait. Although studies during and after the oil fires predicted little long-term harm to people, scientists continue to worry. "The environmental catastrophe that happened to Kuwait is unique. Even though the air is clean now, we still don't know the full impact of this kind of pollution," said lawyer Badria al-Awadi. Cancer in particular may take up to 25 years to develop, so Kuwait's smoky air may yet prove to be deadly. KISR and the Kuwait Ministry of Health continue watching hospital records for signs of trouble today.

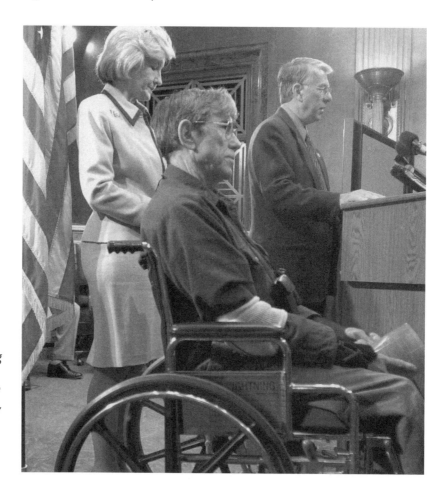

Senator Kay Bailey Hutchison, R-Texas, and Representative Don Manzullo, R-Illinois, have been instrumental in passing legislation helping Gulf War veterans, like Herbert Smith (center), who suffer from Gulf War syndrome. (Photo courtesy of Associated Press)

According to some researchers, these signs are starting to appear. In a 2002 interview, biochemist Lamya Hayat of Kuwait University said that there had been a sharp rise in the number of Kuwait's cancer patients. "Until 1990, we had almost 50 cases of cancer per million people. Now it is in the range of 450 cases per million. Statistically, [that] is a huge increase." Hayat believes that pollutants called heavy metals are responsible. Heavy metals were common in Kuwait's oil smoke.

So far, this link has not been proven. Many other things, including Kuwait's postwar population shift, could have caused a change in the country's health statistics. More study is needed before scientists will understand why Kuwait's cancer rates are rising.

Study and monitoring are also needed in regard to the country's groundwater. Possible contamination will be an issue as long as oil pollutes Kuwait's deserts.

Economic Fallout

Kuwait's oil industry was temporarily crippled by the oil fire disaster. Debts incurred during the environmental cleanup will likely affect the region for decades to come. (Currently, Kuwait has turned to other industries to bolster the economy, as related in the "Moving into the Future" sidebar on the following page.)

The exact cost of the environmental damage is unknown. In 1991 the UNCC was created to process claims from countries involved in the Gulf War. This commission now reports that it has received claims seeking $80 billion in environmental damages. If these claims are approved, Iraq will be required to pay them. Because of the current political climate and Saddam Hussein's fall from power, however, it has become unclear if and when these damages could be collected.

Cleanup funds are desperately needed to clean the oil that still coats the Kuwaiti desert and the beaches and floor of the Persian Gulf. Some funds were drawn from the Gulf Oil Pollution

Moving into the Future

In the wake of the oil fires, Kuwait has rebuilt its oil industry, but it has also begun moving in new directions that will make it more competitive in the current world economy. The government today is working to build telecommunications, information technology, and manufacturing industries. Kuwaiti officials hope that these growing industries will allow the country's economy to stay current with the changing global scene.

Disaster Fund, which had been set up in March 1991 by the International Maritime Organization (IMO). But contributions to this fund totaled only $6 million—a tiny fraction of the hundreds of millions of dollars needed for an effective cleanup—and efforts to raise more money were not successful.

For decades, Middle Easterners have been unconcerned about the health of their land and seas, but that is beginning to change. Some are beginning to speak out on environmental issues. The establishment of Kuwait's Environment Public Authority is one sign that these people are being heard. There is a general feeling that the horror of the oil fires gave citizens and governments a new respect for nature, and today, they also show a growing sense of responsibility for the health of the environment.

Scorched Earth

Throughout history, armies have used *scorched-earth tactics* to destroy the environment deliberately during war, so in concept, the Kuwaiti oil fires were nothing new. In their effect, however, they were acts of ecological destruction on a scale never before seen. The fires did not affect only Kuwait, the intended victim. They also harmed Iraq, Iran, Saudi Arabia, and other countries around the Persian Gulf.

Protecting Earth is difficult when others are determined to damage it. The Kuwaiti oil fires showed the world just how easy it is for one act of war to cause massive environmental damage. They also illustrated that desperate people will do unthinkable things. Before the fires, it was hard to believe that anyone would purposely trigger such a waste of natural resources, but Iraqi leader Saddam Hussein not only took this action, but also threatened to do it again just a decade later. Hussein very well might have carried out his threat in 2003 if opposing forces had not acted swiftly to stop him.

Hussein's actions were a wake-up call. The Kuwaiti oil fires showed the world community that anything is possible during times of war, and they turned the spotlight on scorched-earth tactics in particular. As humankind advances, so does its ability to harm the planet. Governments are increasingly aware that the environment can be used as a weapon. They now know that they must plan ahead to protect their valuable natural resources.

Such planning is especially important for countries that are not as rich as Kuwait—in other words, almost every country in the world. Although the cost was enormous, Kuwait could afford to take care of its worst problems. The country also bounced back fairly quickly from the economic one-two blow of the Gulf War and the oil fires. A less wealthy nation might be crippled for decades by similar events. Green Cross International explained it this way:

> Why should the world care? Natural resources of a country have been hi-jacked and destroyed on purpose, heading to the most important ecological catastrophe of humanity. What happened in Kuwait could happen in any country in the world, and poor countries could never even start to meet the clean-up costs without international solidarity.

CHAPTER 10

Conclusion

A canopy of black smoke hangs above Kuwaiti oil wells that were left intact by retreating Iraqi forces in 1991. (Photo courtesy of Peter Turnley/CORBIS)

There is little dispute that the local effects of the oil fires were disastrous for the region. Particularly in Kuwait, but to some degree in surrounding countries also, the costs of the fires—economic, human, and environmental—were staggering. Although there have been many improvements since 1991, Kuwait still bears the

scars left by its blazing wells. Residents fear that these scars may last forever. "We will never be able to rebuild the Kuwait we once had—the Iraqis and the oil fires have taken that away from us forever," laments one Kuwaiti. From this perspective, it cannot be denied that the Kuwaiti incident was a staggering disaster.

To understand the impact of the Kuwaiti oil fires, it is important to consider the global perspective, in addition to the local view. On a worldwide basis, it appears that the oil fires did little to no harm. Smoke from the fires did not blanket Earth, as some scientists had feared. World climates did not change, and gases from the fires did not poison people in distant lands. Even people who were directly affected by the fires have had fewer health problems than expected so far. These facts point out a positive side to the Kuwait disaster: In many ways, the world got off easy. The results of the oil fires were not nearly as bad as many scientists had expected them to be.

Scientists also feel that it is important to understand how the Kuwaiti oil fires fit into the worldwide pollution picture. Between May 16 and June 12, 1991, scientists from the University of Washington measured and analyzed the pollutants coming from all of Kuwait's burning wells. During this period, the fires released about 2.1 million tons (1.9 million mt) of carbon dioxide per day—only about 2 percent of the worldwide total. The remaining 98 percent came from the normal day-to-day activities of other countries. (Too much carbon dioxide traps heat, and abnormal amounts in the atmosphere would raise global temperatures.) University of Washington scientists also found that the fires gave off about 22,050 tons (20,000 mt) of sulfur dioxide per day. Electric utilities in the United States alone create almost double this amount of sulfur dioxide every day, and hundreds of other countries dump their own sulfur dioxide into the world's air. From this perspective, the sulfur dioxide from the oil fires in Kuwait was just a drop in the global bucket.

A final interesting statistic involves soot and other solid particles. At the height of the fires, Kuwait's oil wells created about 13,230 tons (12,000 mt) of particles per day. Locally, this amount of soot was devastating, because it was so concentrated, but globally, the oil fires accounted for only about 10 percent of humankind's soot output within a year's time. Automobiles and other gas-burning machinery mostly created the other 90 percent.

One might say that the oil fires of 1991 were not confined to Kuwait's deserts. Human civilization's dependence on oil helped create the conditions for this disaster. Oil from Kuwait is burned as fuel in the world's cars, trucks, airplanes, and factories. The flaming oil fountains of 1991 went out long ago, but until the world finds another energy source to replace petroleum, Kuwait's oil fires will continue to burn.

Time Line

1938

Oil is discovered by the Kuwait Oil Company (KOC) in the Burgan oil field

1990

Before the Iraqi invasion of Kuwait, the Organization of the Petroleum Exporting Countries (OPEC) estimates Kuwaiti oil production at 3 million barrels a day

Photo courtesy of Associated Press

August 2   Iraqi troops invade Kuwait; the United Nations (UN) condemns the invasion and demands a withdrawal of Iraqi troops

November 29   The UN Security Council gives Iraq a withdrawal deadline and authorizes the use of force if Iraq does not comply

1991

January 12   The U.S. Congress authorizes the use of military force to drive Iraq out of Kuwait

January 16   Coalition forces launch an air campaign against Iraqi military targets

January 25   Iraq sabotages Kuwait's main supertanker loading pier, dumping an estimated 460 million gallons (1.7 billion l) of crude oil into the Persian Gulf

February 15   Approximately 50 oil wells are damaged or burning, probably due to coalition bombing of Iraqi troops stationed in the area of the oil fields

Photo courtesy of Associated Press

Photo courtesy of Associated Press

February 16–22	Iraqi soldiers destroy hundreds of oil wells across Kuwait, release massive amounts of oil into the Persian Gulf, and sink five oil tankers anchored along the Kuwaiti coast
February 25	Iraqi radio stations announce Iraq's surrender
February 26	Iraqi troops retreat from Kuwait, setting fire to hundreds of damaged oil wells
March 3	Firefighters, including workers from three companies based in Houston, Texas, arrive on the first flight allowed into Kuwait after the cease-fire
March 20	The small crews from Texas manage to bring 20 wells with minor damage under control with equipment found among the wreckage of the war
March 31	Heavy equipment and supplies for firefighting efforts begin arriving in Kuwait at the rate of two cargo planes a day
April 7	A firefighting company from Calgary, Canada, arrives with large tanker trucks that enable firefighters to act as mobile crews; firefighters begin to develop more efficient strategies for fighting the blazing oil wells
April 12	Firefighters have brought 32 wells under control, four of which had been burning
April 22	The emir of Kuwait replaces the minister of oil, fostering better relations between the firefighters and the KOC and leading to more efficient operations
April 25	The first fatality from fighting the oil fires occurs when a reporter's car skids into an oil lake along a road in one of the fields; heat from the car ignites the fumes from the lake

April 26	Sixty wells—20 of which had been blazing—are capped and under control
May	Firefighters begin working on the well called Ahmadi 120, which is spewing 40,000 barrels of burning oil per day; it takes a crew 20 days to bring the well under control; 52 wells are capped
June	Firefighters cap 48 wells; the first tanker to leave Kuwait since Iraqi troops withdrew departs, carrying almost 800,000 barrels of crude oil
July	Firefighters cap 68 wells for a grand total of 245; more firefighting companies from the United States arrive; Kuwait's production of crude oil reaches 140,000 barrels a day, equaling the amount of petroleum the country consumes; the amount of oil leaking from the wells still exceeds production
August	Over four wells a day are capped
September 8	The KOC announces that half of all the exploded wells have been brought under control; the KOC hires firefighting companies from countries all over the world, including China, Hungary, Romania, France, England, and Russia
October	Crews continue to cap wells at an increasing rate; the record is 13 wells brought under control in one day
November 7	The emir of Kuwait celebrates the completion of firefighting efforts in a symbolic ceremony on the Burgan oil field
November 8	The last well, one of the biggest gushers of all, is capped; twenty-four hours after the emir's symbolic celebration, the oil fires are truly extinguished

Photo courtesy of Associated Press

1996

Record profits of $2.9 billion are released by the Kuwait Petroleum Company (formerly the KOC) and its subsidiaries

Photo courtesy of Associated Press

1997

The Shubaiba Refinery becomes the last refinery to reach pre–Iraqi invasion levels of 195 thousand barrels refined per day

Chronology of Fuel Fires and Explosions

The following list is a selection of major fuel fires and explosions of the last 100 years.

1905
Baku, Russia
Oil fire

1937
March 18
New London, Texas, United
States
Gas explosion; 297 killed

1944
October 20
Cleveland, Ohio, United States
Liquid gas explosion; 135 killed

1984
November 19
Mexico City, Mexico
Liquid gas explosion; 334 killed

1989
November 2
Ufa, Soviet Union
Liquid gas explosion; 190 killed

1991
February
Kuwait
Oil fires; 7 killed

1994
November 2
Durunka, Egypt
Fuel oil fire; 500 killed

1995
April 28
Taegu, South Korea
Gas fire; 110 killed

Photo courtesy of Associated Press

1997

September 14

Vishakhapatnam, India

Oil fire; over 35 killed

1998

October 17

Jesse, Nigeria

Oil fire; 1,500 killed

2000

July 10

Egborode, Nigeria

Oil fire; over 3,000 killed

2003

February 18

Whiting, Indiana, United States

Oil fire; none killed

2003

February 21

Staten Island, New York, United States

Oil fire; none killed

2003

September 26

Tomakomai, Japan

Oil fire; none killed

2004

September 16

Lagos, Nigeria

Oil explosion; 30 to 50 killed

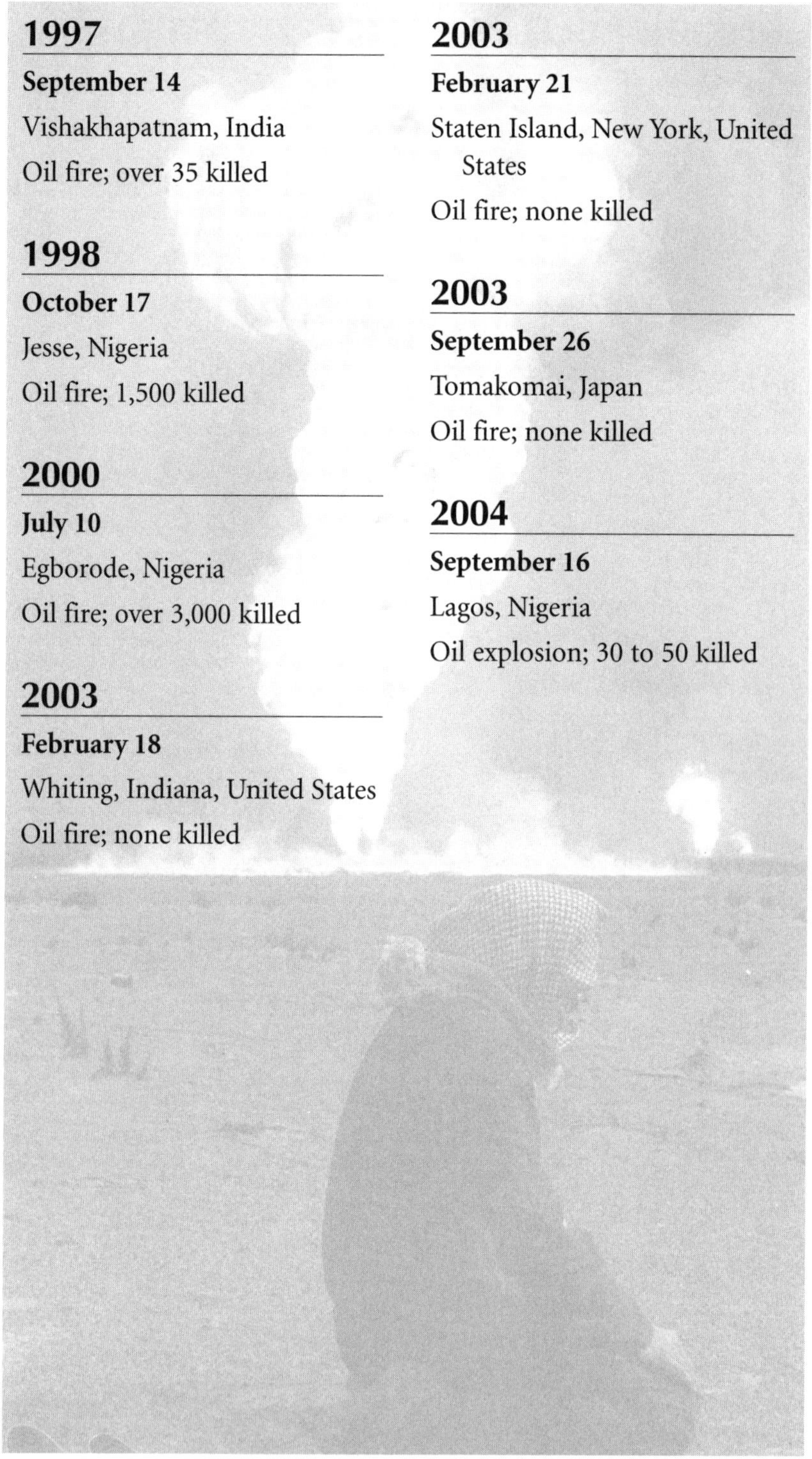

Photo courtesy of Associated Press

Glossary

acid rain   Rain containing acids that form in the atmosphere when pollutants are released into the air

bioremediation   The use of bacteria or plants to remove pollutants in soil or water

blowout   An eruption of crude oil from the ground, usually due to a damaged oil well

booms   Long, flexible, plastic tubes used to contain an oil slick on water

cap   To seal an oil pipeline, such as an oil well, in order to prevent leakage and control flow

crude oil   Oil that has not been treated for usage

dispersants   Chemicals or solvents that break down an oil slick into tiny droplets that quickly sink down into the water

emir   A ruler, prince, or leader

flammable   Easily ignited and capable of burning quickly

fuel   Material that is burned to produce heat or power

ignite   To set fire to

ignition point   The minimum temperature at which something will burn without additional heat

inferno   A place of fiery heat

jet cutter   A tool that emits a high-pressure stream of water and sand, used for cleanly cutting pipes

micron   One-thousandth of a millimeter

Middle East   The area around the eastern Mediterranean Sea, from Turkey to northern Africa, and eastward to Iran

nuclear winter   A worldwide darkening and cooling of the atmosphere theorized to be brought on by large-scale explosions and fires

oil field   A region rich in oil deposits, usually containing working oil wells

oil refinery   A factory where crude oil is processed into fuel for various usages

oil slick   A layer of oil floating on the surface of water

oil trench   A deep cut made to channel oil pools at the height of the oil fires

oil well   A hole drilled in the Earth from which crude oil flows or is pumped

Persian Gulf   An arm of the Arabian Sea between the Arabian Peninsula and southwestern Iran

pipeline   A line of pipes used to transport oil

plume   A cloud of smoke from an explosion that contains pollutants released by the source of the fire

pollutant   Something that contaminates air, soil, or water

reservoir   An underground accumulation of oil

resolution   A statement of intent from a governing body, an assembly, or another formal group

scorched-earth tactics   A military strategy of withdrawing from an area while destroying anything that might be useful to the enemy

self-lofting A process in which soot rises in the atmosphere by heating up the surrounding air

skimmers Boats that suck up or skim oil from the surface of water

tar mat A thin coating of oil that hardens upon dry land

tomography A method of producing a three-dimensional image of an internal structure

toxic Highly poisonous

troposphere The lowest layer of Earth's atmosphere, where all weather occurs

United Nations (UN) An international organization of independent countries established in 1945 to promote peace, security, and economic development around the world

wellhead The top end of an oil well, where oil is extracted

Further Reading and Web Sites

Aerospace Education Center—Fires of Kuwait. This web site gives viewers a fact sheet of important information about the oil fires of Kuwait. Available online. URL: http://www.aerospaced.org/imax/current/fires/facts.html. Accessed August 2, 2004.

Allen, Thomas B. *CNN War in the Gulf: From the Invasion of Kuwait to the Day of Victory and Beyond.* Atlanta: Turner Publishing, 1991. This book discusses the Gulf War and ensuing oil crisis from journalists' points of view.

American Geological Institute (AGI). This web site provides information on geology and tries to increase public awareness of the important role that geological science plays in the use of natural resources and interaction with the environment. Available online. URL: http://www.agiweb.org. Accessed August 5, 2004.

Atkinson, Rick. *Crusade: The Untold Story of the Persian Gulf War.* Boston: Houghton Mifflin, 1993. The Gulf War as seen through the eyes of a journalist who gained access to strategic missions and was on the front lines of the firefighting.

Black, Wallace B., and Jean F. Blashfield. *Oil Spills* (Saving Planet Series). Markham, Ontario, Canada: Scholastic Library Publishing, 1991. This book discusses several environmental disasters involving oil spills, beginning with the Persian Gulf spill. The book provides information on the toxicity of oil to plants and animals, cleanup techniques, and methods of preventing oil spill accidents in the future.

CNN.com/In-Depth Specials: The Unfinished War: A Decade Since Desert Storm—Environmental Impact. This web site revisits Kuwait 10 years after the fires to see the lasting effects of the disaster. Available online. URL:

http://www.cnn.com/SPECIALS/2001/gulf.war/legacy/
environment/. Accessed August 6, 2004.

Elmer-Dewitt, Philip. "Environmental Damage: A Man-Made
Hell on Earth." *Time*, March 18, 1991, 36–37. This article
captured the Kuwaiti oil fire disaster in detail while the fires
were still being brought under control.

The Environmental Literacy Council—Kuwaiti Oil Fires. This
web site is dedicated to helping young people understand the
relevant environmental issues of the day. Contains an
overview of the Kuwaiti oil fires and links to subjects per-
taining to the aftermath of the disaster. Available online.
URL: http://www.enviroliteracy.org/article.php/593.html.
Accessed August 2, 2004.

Environmental News Network (ENN). This web site offers viewers timely environmental news reports. The goal of the
organization is to educate the public about major environmental issues, including actions that people can take in their
own communities. URL: http://www.enn.com/. Accessed
August 5, 2004.

The Goddard Space Flight Center: The Earth Observing System
Project Science Office—Smoke from the Kuwaiti Oil Well
Fires. This site includes information on the Gulf War, pictures of the oil fields taken from space, and news on the
aftereffects of the environmental devastation. Available
online. URL: http://eospso.gsfc.nasa.gov/eos_homepage/
for_educators/eos_edu_pack/p16.php. Accessed
August 5, 2004.

Hawley, T.M. *Against the Fires of Hell: The Environmental
Disaster of the Gulf War.* New York: Harcourt Brace
Jovanovich, 1992. This book describes the efforts to bring
the oil fires under control and the aftereffects of the disaster
on the gulf region.

Holden, Henry M. *The Persian Gulf War* (U.S. Wars). Berkeley
Heights, N.J.: Enslow Publishers, 2003. Fully illustrated with

color photographs, this book gives an overview of the Persian Gulf War. The book includes web links that allow readers to research the topic further.

Horgan, John. "Burning Questions: Scientists Launch Studies of Kuwait's Oil Fires." *Scientific American*, July 1991, 17–20. This article discusses the possibility that information on negative health effects stemming from the oil fires is being kept from the public.

Kuwait-info.com. The Kuwait Information Office web site provides all kinds of information on Kuwait. Available online. URL: http://www.kuwait-info.com. Accessed August 2, 2004.

Kuwaiti Oil Well Fires. This web site has pictures of the burning oil fields of Kuwait. Available online. URL: http://www.fortunecity.com/oasis/niagara/37/kuwait3.html. Accessed August 2, 2004.

Linden, Eugene. "Getting Blacker Every Day: Kuwaiti Oil Fire Fallout." *Time*, May 27, 1991, 50–51. This article, written as firefighters were working to extinguish the flames from the burning oil wells, discusses the threat of the fires' unknown health effects on the Kuwaiti people.

Pars Times—Persian Gulf Oil Fires. This page from an independent web site on the Middle East and Iran displays photos of the fires from the U.S. National Oceanic and Atmospheric Administration (NOAA). Available online. URL: http://www.parstimes.com/spaceimages/persian_gulf_oil_fires.html. Accessed August 6, 2004.

Planetsave.com—"Kuwaiti Oil Fields Offer Grim Reminder of Saddam's Act of Desperation." This Associated Press (AP) article from March 2003 on Planetsave.com gives an overview of the Kuwaiti oil fire disaster and its aftermath. Available online. URL: http://www.planetsave.com/ViewStory.asp?ID=3754. Accessed August 2, 2004.

Press, Skip. *The Kuwaiti Oil Fires.* Buena Park, CA: Artesian Press, 2000. This book discusses the effort to extinguish the oil fires and the environmental consequences of the aftermath.

Pringle, Laurence P. *Oil Spills* (A Save-The-Earth Book). New York: HarperCollins, 1993. The effects of the use of oil on planet Earth are discussed in this book, which includes photographs.

Touby, Frank. "The End of a Firestorm: Firefighters Extinguish Kuwait's Oil Fires." *MacLean's,* November 11, 1991, 46–47. This article, written after the last of the oil fires was extinguished, discusses the economic costs of the disaster.

U.S. Army Corps of Engineers (USACE) Iraq Operations Photos. This web site shows photographs of the fires in Kuwait and the different techniques used to extinguish the burning wells. Available online. URL: http://www.hq.usace .army.mil/cepa/iraq/photos3.htm. Accessed August 5, 2004.

U.S. Environmental Protection Agency (EPA). This is the official web site of the government agency that monitors the U.S. environment. Available online. URL: http://www.epa.gov/. Accessed August 5, 2004.

Zuckerman, Mortimer B. "When it's Dark at High Noon." *U.S. News & World Report,* April 1, 1991, 46. A journalist's experience touring the country of Kuwait after the Iraqis had retreated and the oil fields were set ablaze.

Index